THE HEART'S PORTAL

Awakening God Within
to Navigate Beyond
Great Divide,
INTO NEW EARTH

Zhara J. Mahlstedt

Copyright © 2024 Zhara J. Mahlstedt
The Heart's Portal: Awakening God Within to Navigate Beyond Great Divide, Into New Earth

www.zharajmahlstedt.com

Cover Design by Josué Dersoir

All rights reserved. No part of this publication may be reproduced, distributed, or transmitted in any form or by any means, including photocopying, recording, or other electronic or mechanical methods, without the prior written permission of the author, except in the case of brief quotations with proper citations embodied in reviews and certain other non-commercial uses permitted by copyright law.

To request permission, email connect@zharajmahlstedt.com.

The moral rights of Zhara J. Mahlstedt to be identified as the author of this work have been asserted in accordance with the Copyright Act 1968.

Disclaimer: This book contains the opinions and thoughts of its author and is not intended to provide professional services, medical, or psychological advice. The publisher and author claim no responsibility or liability for loss, risk, or success incurred as a result of the reader's decision to use or apply any of the contents of this book. This book is not intended for making diagnoses, treatment, or cure of any illness or condition. It is recommended that the reader obtain their own independent advice.

Paperback ISBN 978-0-6486199-0-1
Hardcover ISBN 978-0-6486199-1-8
Ebook ISBN 978-0-6486199-2-5
Audiobook ISBN 978-0-6486199-3-2

This book is dedicated to the Ones who have come before, the Ones who will come after, and the Ones who stand here now. It is because of your commitment to reclaim your home that we will witness the greatest unfolding of mankind.

CONTENTS

INTRODUCTION		7
1.	THE NEW EARTH	17
2.	THE ORION WARS	21
3.	THE ROAD HOME	27
4.	RECOGNIZING THE SELF	37
5.	A CHOICE	41
6.	THE GREATEST STORY	45
7.	THE CREATOR	47
8.	RE-EMERGENCE	53
9.	"ORIGINAL SIN"	57
10.	COURSE CORRECTION	63
11.	THE POWER OF APPRECIATION	69
12.	"DEMOCRACY"	73
13.	NO MORE	77
14.	AND SO, IT IS SO	85
15.	THE OPENING	87
16.	HEALING THE HEART	91
17.	THE PORTAL	99
18.	TIMING FORETOLD	103

19.	FORGIVE THEM	107
20.	SELF-DELIVERANCE	111
21.	COMING INTO OUR OWN	117
22.	MANKIND'S BLUEPRINT	121
23.	WITHIN THE WATER	127
24.	SOCIETAL EVOLUTION	137
25.	PEACEFUL PASSAGE	141

CONCLUSION	145
AFTERWORD: ALTERING THE FABRIC OF HUMANITY THROUGH TIMELINE THERAPY	149
APPENDIX: A BRIEF LOOK AT RESTORING THE WATER MOLECULE	155
ACKNOWLEDGMENTS	159
ABOUT THE AUTHOR	161

INTRODUCTION

AWAKENING FROM ILLUSION

Are you waking up?

Twenty years ago, I felt a gentle nudge to open my eyes. I began to read between the lines of the mainstream narrative, gradually realizing that the societal systems in which I had put my trust had been orchestrated for ulterior motives. It was a slow and steady awakening, with each passing year displaying more evidence that what appeared to be a highly functioning, civilized society was actually a grand illusion, with a few masters pulling all the strings.

In those early years, I wished to put my head in the sand and pretend that the world, including its political, educational, medical, and media systems, were just as I had been led to believe — designed to foster goodness within society. My worldview had been constructed on the belief that people did what was best for each other because they were inherently good. I believed that those in authority would always act with integrity.

Discovering that small factions have purposefully manipulated the masses to fulfill agendas driven by greed, power, and inconceivable insidious motives can be a devastating realization, and that's if your ego can come to terms with what has occurred.

If you are brave enough to acknowledge the fact that your "freedom" has been a mere illusion, you open up a life-changing opportunity to cut the strings connected to the puppet-masters and to realign with sovereignty and free will.

UNDERSTANDING THE GAME

As you continue your journey down the rabbit hole after your initial awakening, you may become alarmingly aware that a lack of sovereignty tracks across every aspect of human existence, including the physical, emotional, mental, and spiritual planes. Reclaiming individuality and freedom may become the first and foremost priority, beginning with where you have identified the presence of chains.

However, once you recognize that this reality is an organically orchestrated game that you willingly chose to play in order to have an evolutionary experience as a fractal of Source and that you have always been a cohort to both sides of every coin, then the real awakening can begin.

ADVANCING AWAKENING

Are you ready to remember?

Waking up from the illusion of democracy and limitation can be a more supported and expansive journey if we acquire tools, references, and a comprehensive framework of why we chose to be here in the first place.

Acknowledging that our experience of linear reality on Earth serves as a platform for the soul's development and that the externalized individual and collective worlds mirror our individuated and collective internal states can offer us each a pathway to self-determination and alignment with the resonant frequency of Source, which is unconditional love.

Recognizing the role of the heart's portal in this process is one of the main keys to restoring our innate status as the Creator and freeing ourselves and our society from chains.

THE HEART'S PORTAL

Before we can define the heart's portal, it's important to be aware of the higher heart. The higher heart occupies the etheric realms, is the regulator and integrator of emotional input and output, and understands you, your nervous system, and your entire field of physical reality best.

The higher heart always attempts to steer you in the optimal direction for your soul's highest potential timeline to manifest. It will allow you to make what you may perceive as "mistakes" or undergo "tragedy" so that your growth is catalyzed, and the soul ripens to perfection.

The heart's portal is the layer of consciousness that exists where the physical heart and the higher heart intersect. It is the gateway to Source love, and it is where the soul and the eternal planes of creation reside.

When we open the heart's portal to view from the vantage point of the Source/Creator, we recognize the slave society that we find ourselves emerging from was purposefully designed as a gift by every one of us, including those who sit on the other side of the perceived divide.

Each and every experience presented that does not align with the nature of the heart's love transforms from tragedy into a gift for our self-reflection and growth. This perspective shift dissolves the victim/victimizer reality field and the illusion of separation from others or our highest aspects of Self.

EVOLUTION BEYOND THE HEART

When we dissolve the untruths that we are separate from any other in our reality and cut from Source love, we truly have the ability to create change far beyond mere actions alone.

Reclaiming our innate birthrights as infinite creator beings will propel each of us and our society beyond the lies, deceit, and manipulation that have reigned over mankind for eons, allowing us to unveil a New Earth timeline that has been there all along.

The key to fulfilling our potential as truly unlimited beings in a truly unlimited holographic reality begins with discovering the true nature of the heart.

THE HEART'S GIFT

The heart is at one with the Source, which is the totality of The All, and thus does not live in duality consciousness where there is differentiation between right and wrong, good and bad, dark and light. The heart recognizes the oneness of All That Is, and feels peace knowing that all is well, regardless of the circumstances that may be present.

The heart also knows how to create firm yet loving boundaries for the Self and the Other, taking care of the whole. The heart reclaims balance within the realms of existence in the internal and external worlds as the individual realizes that he or she is The All.

As one comes closer to awakening the heart's portal, all frequencies contained within the individualized Self and the collective whole that are not in resonance with Source love, which is the frequency of New Earth, will be brought to the surface for healing and integration.

At this point, it's critical to understand that if your life is collapsing, people are falling away, or disastrous mishaps or events are occurring in your life or on the Earth, it is all in line with the soul's desire to expand.

Breathe into this space and ask for support when required while you actively participate in your evolution, and as gracefully as possible, hang on for the ride. At this point, you are preparing for a quantum leap in consciousness that will catapult you into your experience of New Earth.

QUANTUM JUMP

The Heart's Portal: Awakening God Within to Navigate Beyond Great Divide, Into New Earth has been written to energetically align the reader with the resonant frequency of New Earth and shares keys that may assist in individual and collective conjunction with this already present reality.

Because time is not linear and all existences overlap in this quantum Universe, it is a shift in frequency within the Self that enables you to interrelate with the essence of New Earth through your own heart's magnificence.

The collective ability to align with a New Earth resonance will come to pass when enough sovereign individuals bring forth their own magnetic resonance as God and hold this force through the storms that may present.

These individuals will know light, dark, and all realms in between and discern everything they see from a transcended state of individuated Source love.

They will have realized they came to play the game, and they will know they have already won because they will understand that they are the Creator.

INTEGRATING THE CREATOR

The experiences that I've had in navigating the three-dimensional and inter-dimensional realms in the last twenty years or so have been many, but it was the merging of my eternal Self into physical form in early 2020 that led me to write this book.

One night around 3 a.m., I awoke, integrating the dimensions beyond time and space into my physical cells, including the memories of The One. With this integration came the ability to harness the free energy that exists in every plane as the latent power of primordial sound reignited within my DNA.

Primordial sound is a form of light language that exists as a quantum encryption in most species' DNA. Not many light languages contain the full resonance of primordial sound. However, primordial sound contains the full spectrum of light.

Light comes in wave or particle form and can be housed within and outside of cellular matrixes. It comprises every living form and all inanimate forms you find in this universal matrix. It is also the matrix.

Light language is a way of profoundly communicating with this light that we are.

LIGHT LANGUAGE

Light language is a broad term used to define languages that resonate at higher dimensional bandwidths than the current languages widespread on Earth. They can communicate with the physical and etheric bodies, souls, DNA, or resonant energy in a space to fast-track healing, awakening, and remembrance. Light languages can also be used to change the vibration of a location or an object, as well as jump timelines completely.

There are many forms of light language, including originations from other galactic species, ancient Earth civilizations, those linked directly with the planetary gridlines, as well as the guiding light from your soul's lineage.

Light language artists can use sound, art, or physical expression to deliver these frequency transmissions.

Everyone has the capacity for light language, but it is up to your soul's evolutionary journey to determine if, when, and in what form it manifests.

PRIMORDIAL SOUND AND ZERO-POINT

The form of light language that I speak is a universal language of love that can resequence DNA. It contains the Source/Creator's original codes, from which we have emerged and are.

The power of this language allows me to harness multi-dimensional energy to create openings in time and space, change timelines, and reorganize harmonics to arrive at the zero-point. I know the zero-point as the void, where everything and nothing simultaneously exist.

The real-time results of primordial sound depend on the intention blended with the zero-point.

When I work with the Earth or the ley lines in the planetary grid, change is seen right away. The energy of density lifts, and the space becomes a portal for whatever intention is set.

I particularly enjoy working with water because it is of pure Source essence. Most of the water on the planet has distortions. Still, it is very easy to shift its molecular structure to resonate purely with the love and laughter of the original Source design.

When people ask for assistance, it is typically their soul's intention and blueprint that supply the information required to support them in creating change in their lives.

Primordial sound opens the doorway for the work to be done quite profoundly, and in the cases of advanced souls and "sleeping masters", it opens the door for them to reactivate their own quantum network to rapidly heal.

The person must follow through with the inner and outer work for lasting change. However, primordial sound will kick-start their genetic awakening, physical healing, manifestations, and/or soul advancement.

DEFINING THE WORD

There are certain phrases throughout this book that are written in primordial tone. They are activating sequences for the DNA and for the consciousness to access the higher planes of creation. They are written to assist you in your own awareness of who you are and to access the infinite state of All That Is. Even though you may not be able to pronounce these sounds succinctly, the energy is imbued upon the page.

Within this book, certain letters and words are capitalized because they are used as signals to remind you of who you truly are. The reference to "YOU" refers to you in your fullest capacity, the YOU that is God.

As we descended through time and space into this Earthly existence, we were wrapped in a false matrix of greed and lies. It was one of the requirements for entry onto this particular planet. If one begins to look into the etymology of the English language, one can begin to clearly see the deceit and the truth of existence that are hidden in plain sight.

The use of the word "mankind" is not meant to alienate women, as we are all "man" regardless of gender. The term "woman" simply signifies "man", with the added differentiation of having a wom(b).

The term "mankind" is used as a catalyst to remove the hu(e) from man and to emphasize the truth that man is a being that was originally rooted in kindness.

The references to Source, Creator, God, The All, All That Is, and The One are used interchangeably to denote the infinite field of intelligence that shapes and is the shape of all universal existence. Simultaneously, you are this Source, this Source is you, you use this Source energy to create, and you are created. The original essence of Source is unconditional acceptance, or, in other words, love.

A VISION FOR RESTORATION

Within this book, I share relevant portions of my personal journey in bridging the divide within my own Self.

Toward the end of the book, I explore several avenues that have been shown to me through the eyes of Source to facilitate the rehabilitation of the Earth and mankind. These suggestions transcend environmentalism, activism, or systemic change, focusing instead on restoring the innate goodness within our society and souls.

I trust that this book will assist you, wherever you may be, on your journey of reclaiming your sovereignty, power, and true identity as love.

Ah siu ta sia tai ah, ah siu tai ah.
May your heart flourish.

1.
THE NEW EARTH

∞0∞

This is the template for The New Earth.

DO YOU HEAR THE CALL?

I write to each and every one of you here at this time of great change, including and especially those who sit in the upper echelons of society, making the calls that differentiate life and death. To those of you in charge of public opinion through your news and media outlets, I write to you, as well as to those in positions of power, whether that be in the form of local, national, or international government. I write to the ones who lend their hands to community, who show up to ensure change is made when the time is ripe.

And first and foremost, I write to each one of YOU, the individuated living being who has decided to come forth onto planet Earth at this time, the YOU that has more power than you could possibly imagine, the YOU that defies time and space and is sitting here writing with me. The baseline template, the blueprint of the human world, is about to change, and all we need to do is keep up.

SHIFTING THE PARADIGM

For too long now, this reality has been driven by mankind's will. Mostly, this will has been taken advantage of, reigned where it was required, and pushed forward by forces with self-serving agendas at play when it was not necessarily the best action for the course of the collective.

Many competing forces have adjusted timelines. Meteors have shifted time and space in an attempt to allow humanity to come into their own, and we find ourselves at a point where the destiny of mankind is at stake.

Despite the chaotic nature of the current world, this period on planet Earth is actually a focal point of goodness and justice, where the old is crumbling and turning head over heels in order for us to see what side is up.

Where do we go from here as a species that has strayed so far from the Creator and his plan? How do we get back on track? Why do we need to? For there is free will...

Why is it a critical period to take free will on board but also to find the easiest access points to shift the time/space dimensional fields into the greatest potential timeline for mankind?

What are we required to see in order to grow through these birthing pains so that we may create an Earth and a universe in which we desire to live?

Right now, we are witnessing the ending of an era and a critical divide in the nature of reality as we see it. It is a point in time where mankind's destiny hangs in the midst of giants, monsters, corporations, and, most importantly, the individuated YOU.

IGNITING THE FLAME

A single person, when the flame of the heart is lit, has more power than one could possibly imagine; when this person steps back into the knowing that they are God, everything changes in his reality and the reality of those around him. When enough of these individuals return to their original Creator state, we will see a rising army large enough to squash any takeover, move through any density, and ensure the original destined blueprint for mankind is fulfilled.

It is written, and it is in the works right now. There are people all over the planet who have the Creator's coding installed in their blueprints. All that we must do is ignite, and when this is done, IT is done. The transition between the old world and New Earth will be complete. It is a timeline that is destined, and now you and I are the ones who are showing up to do the work.

I write to you, the ones who are here to take charge — to break the mold of normality, to transcend the dimensions of time and space, and to help create the Heaven on Earth reality that is currently taking shape.

In the ethers, it builds and trickles down to the planet — step by step, timing exact. There are those who can hold the power of this force and those who get blown over by a gust of wind. Some are here for this journey we are about to embark upon, and some are abandoning ship...more so now than ever.

There is a soul's journey, a soul's pathway to follow. So, fear not, judge not. There is always a rhyme and a reason, and there is, first and foremost, always a season.

In the meantime, we have work to do, my friends.

Let us begin.

Ah siu tai ah, o nai ah?
Are you here to be the change?

2.
THE ORION WARS

My life on this planet has been one hell of a ride. I will start by sharing what brought me here and why I chose to be here at this time, in this dimension, in this body, in this journey we call life.

What I am about to say, though, has no bearing on the truth. All that it does is paint a picture, one of drastic measures, a picture that I share because it will resonate with many of you.

I will tell you why I came here, but I ask you to hold sight of the truth — that we are all One.

You are reading this book to remember, not to forget.

So, as I begin, I say again:

Ka na siu ta sia.

We are ONE.

THE CYCLE OF SEPARATION

I'll tell you about a series of lifetimes I had far away from here and on a different path. One in which my soul was fighting a war in the constellation we know as Orion, far beyond where time and space can linearly take us from here — beyond the Great Divide and into the Great Chasm.

It was hell there. The death toll was atrocious. Not because the inhabitants of this system wanted to die, but unfortunately, there was no choice. Because the warfare had escalated so far out of hand due to the separation that had grown within the fate of many individuated beings, devastation was brought on all. Death was literally the only option.

Separation reigned within the hearts of the individuals. They continued to feed this energy of greed, self-doubt, and internal abuse, breeding an internal and external trajectory of hate, division, and mental patterning of abusers and abused. Due to the consciousness of the majority of individuals, the separation within and between the galactic races of this star system continued to grow.

Time saw truces made between different lineages as they began to recognize the nature of the One, but I did not have the opportunity to see a truce amongst my people.

Death or death were the options, and it always came at a price. The particular solar system I was at home in was laid to ruins, and from the edges of this abyss, we had to find another home, and we had to do so quickly. The air was running out, the atmosphere uninhabitable, and we had no way to survive. So, many of us left. We found a way to escape the devastation and took our remaining families to safety — far away.

This, though, is not why I am writing this book. I am writing to tell you about the possibilities and potentialities that these lifetimes could have held. They could have held magic, but instead, it was mayhem. They could have held beauty; instead, it was grotesque. They could have held the true occupation of a warrior race that had come to peace within its own boundaries, yet it did not.

And so, it spilled over, for the removal of my people did not put an end to war. We took it with us. Over and over and over, we gathered the tribes. We moved, and then we entered battle. It was never truly won, and we moved on again.

Like sheep, we were herded from one pasture to the next, one star system to another, one galaxy away from destruction, always. The battles raged on, the wars were never-ending. Peace was too far from the hearts of the people, and it is for this reason that I write.

UNMASKING THE ENEMY WITHIN

I am writing to you today to ask you to stop. Stop the fighting, for the battle will never be won. It will rage on and on and on. Over and over and over, the cycle will continue if the truth does not surround us, and if we do not find this truth within the very essence of our eternal Self. If we continue to point the finger across the divide, the war will continue, as it rages not from the outside but solely from within.

That is what my people saw. Lifetime after lifetime, rally after rally, hope after hope — it was all extinguished. Over and over and over again, we fought. In times, we won, but truth be told, it was all a loss. It will continue to be so if we do not hold onto the essence of the truth.

The war does not rage from the outside. The guns, violence, drugs, hatred, explosions, and detonations are not because there is an enemy across the line.

It is because we forget that WE ARE the enemy across the line.

WE MUST STOP. I bring you a warning. I come with a simple message. PLEASE STOP. It cannot continue any longer. We must find a way to abandon the ways of the past and move into a future that supports every living being on this planet. The only way to solve the crises that we are in the midst of is to remember the everlasting truth — you are God.

BREAKING THE CHAINS

We are each a particle of God. I do not speak from a religious position; I speak from the space of truth. The truth that was so cunningly covered up to ensure that you would believe the lies.

It was distorted, twisted, and blatantly manipulated to ensure that the war would rage on, to ensure that the people would not know their birthrights, and to ensure that the people of planet Earth would remain part of a slave society until the day they died.

Mankind is collectively a slave to a power so much greater than you may know. You must look beyond the governments, corporations, satanic worshipers, and past the devil himself.

You are a slave to the blindness that you, your Self, have consumed, that you, your Self, have orchestrated and unconsciously agreed to.

You are a slave to the very essence of the root problem that you, your Self, conspired to bring forth into this reality so that you would experience separation.

You are a slave to your misery and your own voiceless thoughts. You are a slave to the eternal wheel that keeps on turning, fuelling the machine in which you take part. You are a slave to the lies that you agreed to when you descended into the vortex of this creationary matrix.

That is...

Until you wake up.

We did not wake up. During my time there at the edge of the abyss, we, as a society, as a great warrior race, stayed asleep. Unaware of the greater truth, we played in the shallows. We stayed out of the deep end, for our knowledge of science was too great. Our viewpoints of how things should be, what works, what is right, and what is wrong were fixed.

We thought not of what could be, but only of what was. As we remained within that framework, we had only one way to go — and that was down with the entire ship.

The energy of our planet was not accelerating. It was not giving birth to a new life as yours is. You have a chance. You have more than a chance; you have a destiny, but it is up to you to hold it, to grasp it, to find it for yourself. The only way that you can devour the truth is to turn everything on its head and not believe one more lie.

WINNING THE GAME

You must find a way to love — to truly love. Not in the sense of a Hollywood romance or the way a mother loves her children. No, this is not the love I speak of. I speak of a love so pure, so clean, so beautiful that not many eyes thus far have been able to see. When one sees this love, one sees the essence of the Creator.

When one sees this true essence, there is no turning back. You can no longer fight; you can no longer call one another names and project violence into the externalized world.

There is nothing more to do, to be, to have.

When you find this love, you know you are God, that you are the Creator.

And when you know this, you have won the game. It is over, and it is sweet sorrow, for saying goodbye to the past has not been easy for the human who has been heavily conditioned by society and the powers that have been.

When we have no more emotions to overcome, struggles to lay rest to, boundaries to climb, and borders to cross, we may feel there is nothing left. We may feel that there is a need to have these challenges because that is what we are used to. Lifetime after lifetime, we have fought. We have brought men to their knees and have been brought to our own.

We have won the wars, and we have lost. We have been the betrayer and the betrayed, the perpetrator and the victim, the accuser and the accused. We have been the one to cause great havoc, and the one great havoc was caused upon.

And yet, we forget this, and still, to this day, we sit there and point the finger at someone else.

Through all of this pain and suffering, we point the finger away from ourselves and blame our losses and our gains on someone outside.

We look at the wars among countries and blame the Arabs, the Israelis, the Russians, or the Jews. We point our finger at the Ukrainians, then take it back again. Before that, it was the Japanese, the Chinese, the French, the Germans, and before you know it, it will be them again. Or maybe this time, it will be the Cambodians coming for revenge.

The enemy is only the enemy within. There is no outside source. It all arises from the true eternal Source of Creation, which is you.

Ah siu ta sia tai ah?
Are you ready to remember?

3.
THE ROAD HOME

YOU ARE GOD

The truth of the matter is that you are God. Truly, the greatest lie that was ever told was that you are not and that you must pray to an outside power to save you.

You are your savior. You are also my savior and the savior of everyone around you because you are a fractal of the whole. A droplet of water in the ocean of life, and just because the droplet has left the ocean, don't for a second think it does not have the power of life.

This fractal, this essence, contains all of the same codes of the Creator himself. This fractal is nothing short of the eternal Source consciousness of All That Is. So, when you decide that the droplet of water across the table from you is just another version of yourself, you will be getting back on track. You will begin to find the answers that you have so desperately been looking for. You will begin to show yourself the road home.

As you find your foothold, as you find the path that leads to your journey of expansion, may you not forget that while there may be pain and while you may experience sorrow, every step of your path is actually gold.

So, fear not; whatever is presented to you is just the path that YOU intended for yourself and your evolution, and it is no mistake. YOU designed it. YOU destined it. YOU asked for it. This road, this time, does not end in destruction. This road, this time, is the road home.

A FORK IN THE ROAD

And so, I write to YOU from this place of destiny unfolded. From this place where I know it is already done, and from this place of watching the Golden Age upon us and knowing quite clearly that it is only a matter of time before we each engage the Great Awakening that is here.

It is only a matter of time before the masses find their edge, their retreat, or their revolt. It is only a matter of time before they stand in front of the powers and structures that be and say, "No more."

And this, my friends, will be their road home.

Yet, for many, it will not be pleasant or peaceful. It will not be an easy ride, so to speak, unless, of course, a different path is chosen.

I propose that you make a choice right here and right now.

Which road are you going to take? The one in which soldiers are marching, oblivious of their forthcoming death? Or will you find the road less traveled — one in which you stand up for the truth? The real truth that you are but a fractal of the Source, and you always stare at a reflection of yourself.

You have a choice here. You can take whatever road you want, as a plethora of options exist. In fact, many have already decided their path. Some are headed down the road of no return — straight to hell.

INTO THE ABYSS

One year ago, my higher Self orchestrated an inter-dimensional journey with a team of astral beings who had access to the plane that we know as the abyss or hell. Little did I know that this journey would change my life forever.

There are multiple dimensions of what we sum up with the word "hell." The one that I accessed is where the eternal flame of the heart is completely extinguished.

I journeyed with a man whose consciousness was already anchored there. Before the passage, I did not consciously understand that I was trying to extricate his soul's lineage from this pit, nor was I aware of the full extent of the journey that I was to undertake. If I had any sense of what was to come, I would have said no.

As I experienced the tortuous existence of this realm, I looked squarely in the face of evil (my twin and yours as well — remember, we are all of eternal Source nature) and asked the entirety of them to come home to their hearts and the nature of the truth.

I asked them to spare themselves the eternal pain that they endured, as the love that I had for those in peril was without discernment or boundaries.

The request was inevitably rejected, and instead, they devoured the parts of me that were within their reach. My soul imprint at that moment changed, for the evil took what it wanted and spit out the rest.

When I had experienced all that I could without a complete fracture of my soul, an army came for me. They were many of my soul's brothers and sisters who sat in line with The One and were prepared for this journey so that I could open my eyes to yet another side of the soul's evolution. They dragged me out kicking and screaming, for I went to recover those lost, and I experienced the agony of recognizing that there was no hope to repair their inner light.

At that moment in time when I knew they were lost, I could not see at all the ones that were saved.

RECONCILING THE FALL

That night of torture was one I will not forget. Yet, it has already dimmed in my life, for the present moment reigns clear. I do not live in a fog of the past, although I do still have my moments of regret.

Why could I not help her? What if I left moments before? What if I said no to the crowd that was asking me to go deep into the pit so that I could deliver a message to the world? Would my entire life not have fallen apart?

These are the standard questions we all pose to ourselves during moments of unclarity. I had mine branded on my forehead for months. Why did I go, and what did I actually retrieve?

At the time, my answer was "nothing."

And so, for months afterward, I recovered. Set free of all of my duties to heal the wounds and find space in nature where I could sit and be still so that the fractures within my soul could be repaired.

Why did I go, I would ask? Not only did I lose those there, but I also lost myself. I forgot the truth of the matter — that the ones who had fallen had planned their execution. They had planned their arrival to that moment in time specifically so they could find their remembrance.

They chose that path, and whilst I may have wanted to, I could not change it for them. It was not my job and never was.

Some choose a harder road than others, and for these people, we cannot mourn, for they have chosen, and our Universe is one of free will. While we may want it to be different, we must surrender to the fact that the darkness is but a shadow of the light, and in darkness, there is also truth.

Yet, as I write these words, and I know their truth, I cannot help but wish it was another way, for the suffering is extreme. It is beyond what I am able to describe with words, but like the excruciating pain of most childbirths, the horror has dimmed.

I entered and sat with them, beyond the confines of time and space, in the pit, the eternal depths of hell, and saw and felt a version of reality that I wish I could forget. The torture of the soul is relentless, and the depths of pain are chasms beyond what one could possibly fathom.

Unlike a nightmare, this is real, in full color, without filters; it's pure torment beyond these gates. There are souls fractured beyond repair. And yes, they hold the fort; yes, they hold the flame — burning from a very different angle so that we may see our way home, as they, too, are just another version of the eternal One.

Not everyone has to suffer. Not everyone has to take the road home through the darkest depths of despair; not everyone has to have eternal damnation at their doorstep.

There are many other ways. However, many of you had already decided before you entered this reality field that the experience you wanted was either of the dark or of the light. You knew what you were in for, and you said, *"hell yes, I'm doing it this way!"* because you knew that would be the greatest gift that you could offer mankind. My sisters and my brothers, we need this experience, and that's why you choose this woebegone path.

We must expand; we must come for these depths (dark) so that we can rise to these heights (light).

And to those who have made this choice, I salute you, for it is not one that I would make. I would never go there again, not for one moment, as the suffering is unbearable, the darkness and distortion is enough to swallow you up whole.

To you, who may be faced with critical choice in your path's unfolding, please consider this — there is another way.

THE GOLDEN ROAD

The golden road knows the middle ground. It looks at the darkness as well as the light and loves them each as they are. It knows that the existence of duality is also the truth of the whole.

Without judgment, without scorn, this golden light of Source sees the true nature of All That Is.

It is a love that knows no boundaries, that has no ends, that looks beyond the veil of separation and sits at the table with kings and paupers, angels and demons. This love is not earthly. This is the love of the Creator, and this love would never abandon anyone, not one being on this planet we call Earth.

The Source/Creator does not judge one as a sinner or saint, and leaves discrimination for the Earth-bound minds.

You can have destroyed villages filled with children and crying babies, and God will still be there. There is no pain that God cannot fix. There is no sorrow that God cannot heal. God never abandons you, but instead leaves room for you to rise and fall, just as you shall. God sees all, hears all, and is all.

Before you fall on your knees in prayer to an entity outside, let me be really clear. God is you.

The energy that creates worlds, the essence of this very moment, is all God. The words on this page, the breath that we breathe, the moments of stillness and the moments of slaughter. It is one and the same…it is God.

So, there is no need to condemn nor judge anything that you see within or without. Because when you judge or condemn, you are looking at yourself and inflicting the biggest dividing chasm that you could possibly imagine, and it hurts both the Self and the Other.

YOU ARE THE FORCE OF GOD

Come back with me, please, to the very moment in time in which we were born, in which we gave birth to creation — this was experienced by each one of us. This wasn't some outside source. This was YOU. It was always YOU.

> God is not a separate entity.
> God is the life force, the blood that runs through your veins.
> God is the passion and the almighty sword.
> God is the good, the bad, and the ugly.
> God is the force of all creation, and that force remains in each one of you.
> Do you hear these words? The force of God runs within you. It is YOU.

You are an electrically charged system in an electrical body that has made this Earth plane your home, for now. You are a walking circuit board receiving and transmitting signals twenty-four seven because of the brilliant electrical charge that is innate within all beings. It may look different from species to species, yet encoded in all are electrical components that defy the densities here on Earth.

No landline or satellite phone is needed for your communication with the beyond. It is literally a multi-wave radio machine that YOU are. You are an electromagnetic transducer and transceiver, conducting the energy of various forms and currents through a physical vessel, the body, which is predominately water.

You are coded in circuits, in programs, in deceit and lies too, because, of course, they told you that you were "just human."

They told you that you had no power and that you must stay locked up in your house so that you did not get ill.

They told you that war raged on in Afghanistan, Ukraine, Iraq, Jordan, Gaza, and the Sudan, and that you had no control. You had no effect and no power over these circumstances. They told you millions were dying and that they were victims of circumstance. They told you that innocent bystanders were slaughtered due to actions of evil forces that you could not prevent.

THEY LIED.

YOU are the greatest gift that has come to this Earth.

YOU are the force that can change it all.

YOU are the darkness and the light, the alpha and the omega, the beginning and the end.

YOU are the entirety of the Universe wrapped up in one body.

YOU are the match that lights the flame, and you are the flame.

YOU are The One/Source/Creator of All That Is, and YOU have the power to change everything.

Are we clear? You were lied to, and it's time to hear the truth.

You are God.

A RESET OF THE HEART

Lifetime after lifetime, I have been exposed to the brutality, the servitude, and the unending battles that have made up the human race. I have also seen goodness and greatness. I have seen the beauty and the magnificence of the creatures of this planet, and I am in love with this place I call my Earthly home.

But all in all, the human race is a dying breed that requires a reset. A reset not of the mind, the brain, or the entire quantum soup that we live within, but a reset of the heart.

So, I invite you to walk with me to find the space where you can truly see the wheat from the chaff, the forest from the trees, and the existential crises that rest within humanity's collective psyche. I invite you to walk with me and find the answers to these crises not in another but only in the Self.

When one takes this path, one finds the road home.

And my friends, we must abandon ship, or we must bring it through the darkness. There is no other way. Your only lifeline is to go within, for here is where you will find the savior that you have been looking for.

It will not come from your governments, political leaders, or even your spiritual ones. It will not come from your father, sister, partner, or your best friend. As much as we cling to those around us, we must let go, for they are not our lifeline. We are our own lifeline, and salvation will only come from the truth — that you are a fractal of the One, and in this, you are all things.

Ah siu ma sia tai ah, o mai ah?
Are you ready to realize who you are?

4.
RECOGNIZING THE SELF

THE ORIGINAL EXPERIMENT OF LIFE

I arrived on this Earth eons ago to scout this planet for conditions that would support life. Life has been an ongoing experiment, for the day we formed as cellular organisms in the womb was not our first. Many of you, like myself, have been instrumental in the ongoing experiment that is life.

We "sat around the table" in another dimension, unlike our current one, and wondered how we could continue to experience the great unfolding that had been set forth. We wondered what it would be like to create an organism that could sit, talk, breathe, and have experiences in conditions so far from our own that we wouldn't even recognize our own Self.

We did a good job in that respect. We succeeded. We made a universe so vast, with such scope that we could not fathom the potential outcomes, and this is how war came to pass. The undesired and unseen result was that we would stray so far from our truth that we would need to launch a rescue mission to recover our inner knowing that we were the creators of this reality and the Creator of the Universe as a whole.

Do you know who you ask for when you ask for God? Or when you ask for your angels to come online and support you? Do you know who you ask for when you call upon your medicine men or your shamans?

You are calling for your true Self to emerge. You are not looking for the savior in another. You are not looking for the answers in another being. You are looking for the truth to be reflected to you, that you are the greatest Source that has ever lived.

You forgot your way, and I forgot mine. Now, here we stand on the precipice of Great Divide, and we have a choice. It's either up or down, sink or swim.

CHOOSING THE GOLDEN AGE

The eternal planes of creation hold their hands out to us to return home. We have the choice to take the doorway that has opened in front of us or to turn a blind eye, pretend that we don't see it, and walk the other way. The doorway is opening for all of us, and we get to choose which of the myriad of paths we will take. Simply stated, are we going home, or are we going to hell?

Hell is not a space that one may want to embrace if one wants any sense of comfort. And yes, it has been set in motion by the forces that require our separation to maintain control; however, these beings, too, are only a reflection of the greater sum of the parts. They, too, are God.

You may not want to recognize that truth. While you may want to stare evil in the face and call it by its name, consider a view beyond the veil and the darkness that it is enshrouded in and call yourself back to your heart. For the darkness is only another version of you.

This does not excuse the injustices of the world, but if we continue to look through the same lens, we will get the same result. I have had enough of witnessing the same result repeatedly, which has led to lifetimes of war, devastation, and suffering on this planet, as well as many others. I ask you to consider a different viewpoint. I invite you to construct the vision that you see in front of you as one that is not evil, good, trapped, free, light, or dark.

I invite you to choose the line of sight of the heart. It transcends judgment of yourself, others, or the state of the experiences you find yourself in. This is the internal beacon that will guide you back to the Golden Age — the days that have long since passed and that are destined to return. The days that are ready to reappear on this planet are like nothing that our human eyes will remember. I ask you to remember from the core of your being the essence of your Self that I speak of, for it is time for these days to return in all of their beauty, magnificence, and radiance. It is time for our planet to experience Heaven on Earth.

And yet, it has been here all along. We have just been blinded by our ways, our limited perceptions, and our intrinsic beliefs. We have sat in the shadows, basked in the light, seen the divide, and focused our eyes here.

ENDING THE WAR

I invite us to refocus our gaze on the life that many of us were born to live. A life in which the human reference point shifts from the "I" to the ever-expanded version of the Self. A life that sees no harm in any of the destruction, sees no violence on television, and sees nothing but the beauty of the life force within the being in front of them, regardless of who they are.

I invite you to refocus upon the truth and to shine the light on the oneness of all creation. Shine the light into the darkest recesses of the soul and recognize that darkness as the most beautiful version of you. I invite you to recognize that the darkness and the light must co-exist for the battle to be won. The integration of the fields of consciousness is vital to regain control of the battlefield and put an end to the war.

Again, I remind you the war does not rage outside. The war is fought from within. The outside war that you see is only but a manifestation of your own Self, and your own Self is merely a reflection of mine. With this ability to see the truth, you would never have to worry again, for you would know that you would never abandon yourself. You would never take yourself anywhere that you could not return from, and you would know that you were exactly on the road home.

When you find the path, when it lights up in front of you, you will be able to see it for what it is — the ever-expanding version of the Self in manifest form.

Let me remind you once again you are God. You are the Creator in manifest form, here to grow through experience, as are the brothers and sisters that find themselves also located at this point in space/time.

So, when you see them from this point onwards, can you look at them with new eyes? Can you see them for the ever-expanding versions of Self that you also are? Can you see them for the truth of the being that they are? Without judgment, shadow, darkness, and without "truth," your "truth" that they are separate beings, in separate bodies, on separate journeys, and that they do this or that to you.

Put this story down no matter how great, and you will see the world change in front of your eyes.

Ah nai ah na, siu nai ah, siu ma sia.
Are you ready to come home to the heart?

5.
A CHOICE

THE JUDGMENT ERA

Writing from the space in between, I see an outdated story that has percolated to the human form, that is, in a sense, only another version of every story ever told.

It is the story of separation, and it lives within you as a packet of information stored within your cells' genetic structure until you find the space in between and create from the heart.

The story of separation goes back to a land before time, to a space in our history files that we no longer remember. It was our decision as the One to ride a wave of duality to experience the different wonderments of life. The initial decision was not judged as bad; in fact, we wanted to play in all realms. It was an open-ended adventure! The mind was the one that took this split perspective and delineated good from evil, bad from worse, yes from no, and everything in between.

The judgment era began, and so did the stories, and these stories evolved into war in all of its various forms. You do not require guns to fight, nor sticks or stones. You can enter war with your breath or thought forms alone.

As your mind forms judgments of yourself, others, or situations of a critical nature, you are uttering vibrations that feed the polarity structure set within our Universe and your own Self. It is a maneuver away from Source rather than back to eternal love.

THE BIRTH BLUEPRINT

Are you sick of the pain that this torment of division produces? Are you ready for a fresh start in which you integrate the pain and suffering through your heart's portal so you may build your bridge to New Earth?

When we view another as none other than God, we begin to embody the expanded nature of the Self. We see the truth of the reflection that stares us in the mirror — that we are the Creator, as is every brother and sister that walks down the street.

This is our family, and we ceased to recognize them as so due to the very nature that was inflicted upon us at birth. The birth blueprint of separation and strife was deeply embedded within the human genome, and life was enshrouded in an air of poverty or lack, although there are occasional ones who have cracked the code. Within the majority of the humans on this planet, separation still prevails. When separation prevails, lack of some form or another will be displayed.

When lack of consciousness is present, it plays out as the stories of our lives, in our livelihoods, relationships, health, and/or physicality. In one way, shape, or form, the genome reflects the imprint that was given to us at birth — that of separation. Fear not; we, as One, are working on solutions as we speak. For every problem, there is always a solution. For every yin, there is a yang. And for every question to the Universe, there is a vibrational match that returns.

So, we need not be disturbed by this gene of separation that has plagued human existence for eons; however, we must be aware if we would like to begin to make different choices for our journeys.

Not every being is creating wars and perpetuating pain within the lives of others in humanity, but to some degree, most are contributing to the devolution of the species purely from separation-based thought forms and the inability to recognize the Other as the Self.

Remember, the genome was tampered with in the early days, so we cannot blame ourselves or anyone else for these loops that we run on. It is what it is, and it is why this game of separation is so prevalent in today's society. Because at the very core of our cellular makeup, we have been given an altered gene code to ensure that the separation continues. When we know this, we can consciously use the mind to choose a different route.

GAME OVER

Let me suggest that we give up the game, one step at a time or in one fell swoop. The choice is yours, but if we truly wish to see the evolution of a species, the game of separation must be relinquished first within one's Self, then with his/her relationship with others and the world.

Love yourself for who you are, not for who you are not. Be with each other for the pure joy and celebration of life and put down the story of betrayal and hurt at another's hands. For truly, this is the gift that they are giving you — the ability to be at one with the Creator by showing you where you are not.

When you are triggered by another being or situation in your hologram, this is the point of choice in which you can continue to buy the game of separation or high-five your eternal Self and the Other for creating a brilliant situation for each to grow.

Do we opt for the first choice and look externally to blame, judge, and perpetuate the cycle of shame? Or do we look internally to address the pain that is creating the reaction and recognize the incredible gift that is being given so we may move through this phase of evolution?

There is nothing else to ending the game other than recognizing the framework of the matrix for what it is and slowly but surely implementing steps to turn in the direction of your eternal heart's desires.

Each moment is but a choice, and it is yours.

Siu ma sia tai ah.
You have got this.

What gifts are presenting as pain?

6.
THE GREATEST STORY

∽∾∾

The greatest story ever told is that you are the Creator.

When you descend from the eternal greatness of the Source, you are known as a fractal, a descendent, the greatest gift of all time, with all the capabilities of the Creator. Do you remember yet?

This book is also to help you remember your power as God. As you find your power, we will find ours, and there will be no greater gift that we can give each other than to remember who we are.

This has been foretold in the greatest prophecy that there ever was — that you would find God and return home to the eternal essence of the Self through the heart's gifts.

As a result, you would once again build a civilization of greatness that would strike fear into the minds of men who had not yet come running for the heart's light. And so, they would attack, and attack they did. Running straight at you with their Bibles and their chains to ensure you believed you had to be under their control and under their roof in order to find God and salvation.

There has been no greater lie in the history of mankind, and you are about to uncover the truth. You are about to set fire to the book that has held you and the chapters that were written to ensure your history was sealed. You are about to turn the page and find the greatest story that was ever written.

This story is YOU.
You are not what you were told.
You are God.

Siu ma sia.
I see you.
Ah siu ta sia tai ah, ku mai ah?
Have you remembered me?

7.
THE CREATOR

∞0∞

THE GREAT HARMONIC HUM

Let us start from the beginning and from where it all fell apart. The Creator of All That Is wanted to experience life. This Creator was an energy field so vast, so voiceless, so unusual that the words in the human dictionaries do not have accurate vocabulary to describe who and what this Creator was.

It is all contained in the sounds of the great harmonic hum that set alight the great unfolding that you are here to witness.

Let me share with you through this particular recount.

"In the beginning was the Word, and the Word was with God, and the Word was God." John 1:1

Not all of the Bible is a lie. In fact, the truth remains, hidden behind distortion so that the masses lined up at the altar as they walked through the doors on Sunday.

Have you read between the lines?

Once upon a time, there was a force so great that only the Creator could hear it. He was in an echo chamber uttering only sounds of the Self.

Translated through the universal dialect of primordial sound, I know the words to be these:

Ah siu tai ah, o nai ah.
Ah siu tai ah, ai ah nai ah.
Ah siu tai ah, o siu nai ah.
Ah siu tai ah, siu mai ah.
Ah siu tai ah, ah siu tai ah, ah siu tai ah.
Ku mai ah.

He was speaking only of his heart, of the great heartbeat that would give rise to mankind. And not just mankind; the greatest galaxies that have arisen have been through this breath. And not just the greatest galaxies, but the uni (one) — verse (song, praise) as a whole.

It was all spoken through His Word, the original sounds of creation.

For those of you who I may be losing, let's come back to a simple fact that your science will validate. Sound translates to vibration, and vibration shapes matter.

What if these sounds of resonance of the Creator's heart catalyzed not only the Earth and all who walk upon it, but gave way to the sounds that shaped the entire uni (one) — verse (song, praise)?

What if these original sounds were sung in such a manner so that the vibrations connected with the ethereal planes and created a landslide, one that could not be stopped? Where matter was put into motion, and life itself took off, springing forth? What if the intention that was added with these sounds came to give rise to new life specifically because this Creator had it in his thoughts to merge with the oneness of All That Is?

THE COSMIC PLAYGROUND

What if this Creator needed an outlet, a space to be, breathe, dance, hold, and be held? What if this Creator wanted a space to play and someone to play with? Many someones. Would this Creator replicate himself time and time again to become a form in which he would dance with his reflection?

What if this Creator's original intent was to play? What would you think then? Would you think our wars, our current duties to Self and to each other, were on the mark?

Would you think that you were doing life "right," or would you make some changes? For the joy that is within the Creator is also inside of you.

The Creator came to experience himself in all of his glory, in all of his joy, in all of his expansion. And yet, how could he know this version of Self if he knew not the opposite? He required a reference point. If one does not know dark, how does one know light?

And so, the original concept must be unveiled — that this all was a divine creation from the start. Birth, death, hate, love, joy, despair, good, and evil were all set up as constructs so that he could find his way home, back through the heart. The Creator treated it as a divine game of infinite intelligence that could continue to grow far beyond the original bounds that were intended. As the game grew, linear reality took form.

TIMELINE JUMP

We find ourselves in a linear experience, but the truth of the matter is time is anything but. And so, we find our way into the discussion of the radical, of the unseen, of the unspeakable, for it is time to get real.

What you see is not what you get, at least not always. You have a choice. At any moment, you can choose a different latitude, angle, or position, and not just with your words, attitudes, and thoughts.

You are the Creator, and you can change anything and everything at will, including this distorted reality we now find ourselves in.

Do you know that when enough of us find ourselves with the ability to warp time and space, we will make a decision collectively to birth the New Earth?

This time/space dimension will shift so radically, with only one thought of the collective mind, that we will alter the course of history and mankind as a whole.

ALL ROADS LEAD HOME

Yes, we will still have those who have made their choices to go into the depths, 20,000 leagues under the sea, so to speak, and the water will not be inviting. And this space I speak of, I will speak of no more, but as you navigate your life, please hold this true. You cannot save them all. You are not here to save them all. You are not here to guide them all to mankind's future destiny.

You are here to lead the way for a few hundred thousand, a few million at most. And the rest you let go, and you suffer not in this knowledge, as it is not failure. It is a destiny already pre-determined. We each made our own choices. We each chose our path. We were told we had options, and yet, someone had to go to the depths of hell, to the abyss, to ensure the path was paved with good intentions so that we would eventually find our way home to the Source. And home we will find, whether it is sooner or later, we will each return.

The slaughter of a thousand men does not come without repercussions, and some may choose the path that entangles. The entanglement of the cords through the death process must be cleared, and like the karmic cords that bind, so does death.

So, you find your way, one way or another, to the knowing that you are God — that we each are the way, the truth, and the life. And yes, for some, this does involve suffering.

Do not take upon yourself the burden of responsibility that you could have done better, that if you had only done this or behaved like that, life could have been different for many, for it would not have been. It can only shift from your present stance (presence). So come back here, right now, and let us find the road home.

Ah sia tai ah, siu ma sia
The road home sits here in the present.

8.
RE-EMERGENCE

∽o∾

LOVE AND LAUGHTER

Have you found yourself in a space where you know you have more to accomplish than sit on the sidelines and watch this great unfolding?

Have you once in a while thought that there may be more to this life?

Have you ever wondered if it could be nothing more than a game, similar to the video games people play or the ball fields that are lined with spectators?

Have you ever thought, *Okay, there are two sides, which one will I choose?*

This game is not about choosing a side or about taking a stance. It is not even about finding the Self. Surprisingly, it is only about having a great time. The Creator wants to laugh and love. He wants to be present again in an era where harmony reigns, where peace prevails, and where he comes back to the eternal truth of existence through our experiences.

He wants to be free to be the sovereign and respected individual that he is. He wants to be present as the One, and he wants to experience that through YOU because he is YOU.

There is no delineation or line in the sand. There is only one truth: that you are the Creator and that you have all that you require to find your way home.

The essence of the eternal lies within the seat of the soul, and the heart space re-emerges to awaken the tribes of mankind back to their destiny course — to be free to choose the life that they want to live. If this is one of harmony and laughter, so be it.

PURPOSEFUL PROGRESS

While we are re-engaging these memories, we must be swift, for time as we know it is running out.

This is not to put undue pressure on your soul's journey. It is just a nudge to keep going. Do not doubt the path that you walk. Keep your sights aimed high. Keep your focus centered. Keep your goals first and foremost in line with your highest purpose and path.

SHAPING THE PRIMORDIAL SOUP

Do you know how intention affects the timeline on which you play?

Each and every time you have a moment of thought, a moment of feeling, you open a new doorway or close an old one. Your intention runs deep in every moment, into the eternal gateways of time and space.

What does your intention have to do with your reality, you may ask?

This is a primordial soup, the reality stream in which you live, and there are infinite buttons upon which you can press. Each moment in time, there lies an infinite ability to make infinite choices.

Do you see your greatness?

This is YOU, the Creator of your destiny, the rockstar of your world. You are the one on the stage, and you are the one who controls the music. You have the ability to shape time and space as you know it, more so than you can possibly imagine.

So, let us come up to speed.

EMBRACING OUR GIFTS

When we are told we have a mission on this planet, especially in this time, we can either ignore it, or we can step up. Let me tell you, I have ignored it time and time again. I thought all along that I was on track, on point, playing the human identity to the best of my ability, rolling with the punches, and shifting the egoic nature to the blueprint that is of the Creator.

I have done well, but until the day that I began to write, I missed the entire point of the journey. When one has a gift, and that gift is ready to express, one gives it the leeway to be set free.

Like so many of us, I have wanted to stay hidden, tucked away where no one would know who I was or what I brought. So much so, in fact, that I have diminished myself to not even fully embody my own truth in this very moment.

Yes, I know. Yes, I see. Yes, I am highly aware. Yes, I remember.

But do I really know? Have I embodied this truth beyond what I currently think to be the way?

That remains to be seen.

What is your gift to give to this world? What is your role? How can you be of service to yourself and to those around you?

YOUR ORIGINAL EXPRESSION

When you decided to manifest in physical form, you knew that you would be a part of this great tapestry called life. You knew that it would be rich with experiences galore, and you knew that you may not like them all. But in this knowing, you recognized that you would find your way through a sharp point of pain, and you would use this growth to catalyze growth for others.

You also knew that it could be a bumpy ride as the majority of you reading this were ready to take on a great amount of pain for mankind so that you could pull them out the other side.

This old-world pattern of acclimatizing to mankind's suffering has run its course. It is not your job to save anyone, nor are you here to be saved. It is your job to get in line with what you originally intended when you decided to set the course for Earth — to find the center point that is the heart.

When you find this point, the true gift that you are here to give the world will shine. This is how you will alleviate pain, as the joy of your original expression will brighten every person that you meet.

Siu tai ah, Siu tai ah, Siu tai ah.
Will you let your heart grow?

9.
"ORIGINAL SIN"

THE VOID

I was standing on the top platform of a uniquely crafted wide, wooden slide in the middle of a playground at my Baptist primary school when I saw my first glimpse of the truth. Eyes wide open, all of a sudden, I was just there. I entered the fields of creation and was intensely present in the void, that great unknown in which all things exist, and yet nothing does, all at once.

The feeling was one of calm, peace, and complete surrender; yet a charge of intense energy filled the air.

I saw only dark but knew only light, and here in the space-in-between, I knew I was home.

How did I get there? I do not know. It just happened. And when it happened, I knew there was much more to life than I could possibly imagine.

PROGRAMMED DUALITY

Yet, the programming set in thick during my early years as a child, and the trauma was great, as it is for so many of us as we descend upon this planet.

Every day for nine years, the Baptist religion disseminated the belief that God lay outside of me and the only way to be saved was to go to church and pray.

I spent every day in anxiety and fear. Did Jesus hear me when I asked him to come into my heart? I asked every night because each time I asked, there was no feeling that he did; nothing changed.

I feared my father would not go to heaven because he did not believe in God, and because the framework was of heaven and hell, I feared he would descend into horror. At least my brother was in Baptist school, so while he may have acted more like a sinner than a saint by church standards, at least he had a chance.

And my mother, well, I was not so sure that God would take her to heaven when she did die because I was being taught by the Baptist religion that she was betraying the one true God. She was looking to all religions for the truth as she was aware her time on the Earth would soon be coming to an end.

I would peek through the bedroom door, watching her chant with a Buddhist friend in front of an altar. It gave me an inward panic attack that she was not worshiping the only God that mattered, the one I was told was the right one.

It confused me as my mother ought to know what she was doing. Perhaps it was the cancer that made her turn away from the only God that mattered. Or perhaps it was because that God was not helping her. If this God was not helping her, then was that God the right God?

The amount of stress that compounded upon me as a child growing up in a Baptist school is not something I have actually recognized until this moment in time as I write.

The dichotomy between good and evil, right and wrong, and truth and lies was the only thing I knew. Free thought, free speech, and freedom of worship were not tolerated. You got in line, or you got out. And so, the programming set in hard and fast from the time I was five.

Let me please take a brief sidestep from the bottom line and note that the people at this Baptist school were the most caring, kind-hearted, loving group of people that I could have known at the time, for they truly did care. When my mother did pass when I was ten, they banded together and cared for my brother, father, and myself in a way that most other communities would not.

Brainwashing is brainwashing, though, whether we like it or not, and all belief systems do just that.

FITTING THE MOLD

So began the earthly journey to fit in. To be right, not wrong — always. My entire life on this plane has been trying to fit into the mold even though the Universe always conspired to ensure that I would never do just that.

My mother, who was from Taiwan, maintained her language and cultural identity the best she could. Growing up, it clashed with my deepest desire to look, dress, and act like the girls I carpooled to school with, who were blonde-haired, blue-eyed, stylishly dressed, "normal" American girls. If someone had told me then how special it was to be different, perhaps I would not have spent another thirty years trying to fit in.

THE MASCULINE AND FEMININE DIVIDE

When my mother passed away, I was ten, and it was just another notch on the belt of feeling alone. Not only because of her death but because I felt God could not be real. With so many prayers from so many people, why did my mother die? It was the first feeling of betrayal.

The second feeling arrived when I overheard my father tell a friend that before my mother passed, she was calling to him, but he did not go to her and had instead chosen to continue on his task at hand. He did not know what was to come.

There was a sense of deep betrayal between the father and mother figures. It was my first taste of the relationship between the masculine and the feminine, not that at that early age I could possibly understand the deeper meaning, but it set into motion a pattern in my life of separation. Not that I did not have beautiful relationships with the opposite sex, but there was always some sort of falling away or betrayal of sorts, and it always had to do with me.

I did not know what it meant to be loved, or how to give or receive love. Love was always clingy in some way, with an undertone that I needed a man to love me to prove my worth. In truth, I was always happier when I wasn't in a relationship. However, when the opposite sex was involved, I would always feel this underlying current of need manifesting it in my life.

This need went much deeper than the typical desire to find a partner to be whole, as did the experience of betrayal. What Source has relayed to me in these recent years is that in the deepest recesses of time, there was an instance in which the feminine and masculine energies split and no longer functioned from union. This undercurrent is present in our lineages today.

The divide was created when the original fractals of Source were produced — one masculine energy and one feminine. Simply stated, it was when these polar opposite energy fields comprised of magnetism and light were created that the "original sin" occurred.

"Original sin," as it is known, was never a negative event, nor was it associated with guilt or shame. The original fall from the original state of One was a choice, a conversation piece, and an adventure! There was never any form of judgment around the abandonment of the original form of Self.

It just was.

FRACTURED IDENTITY

When One became two, these fractals created a cataclysmic shift in the nature of the hologram that not even Source knew was going to occur, as it was the first experiment with removing himself from the original state of One. As he became two, a split in the nature of identity formed, and he felt the hollow shell of each form.

There was not nearly enough grief to abandon the experiment, but there was enough of a distinct resonance of lack that it gave him cause for concern that his experiment may need to be abandoned as future generations played out.

The experiment was designed to carry him away from One into two and see how far he could split without losing sight of his true identity.

One became two, and eventually, two became three. From there, we see the story of the Holy Trinity expand into a lineage that would eventually lead to the nature of the hologram that we have today — identities so fractured that they do not remember that they are the same Source.

This original rift carried through the generations and manifests in the individual cellular state of many who reside in this universal realm today.

This was a lineage carved from this separation from the very get-go. So, when we look at healing ancestral lines, we must go back further than seven generations. We must go back to the land before time, where we can recognize the greatest truth was always right in front of our eyes. You are a reflection of me.

SIN'S GIFT

The gift of "original sin" sits with us every day. If we did not know separation, how could we possibly know wholeness? The game was always designed to point back to the original blueprint — and that is YOU. You, just like me, are the way, the truth, and the light.

"Original sin," when turned on its head, is one of the greatest gifts we have known. Without this origination point, we would not have had the opportunity to play. We can create from this experience of duality a very different point of view that can lead to a drastic shift in the nature of our individualized and collective hologram.

Are you ready to look from the eyes of Source and expand into a view that will bring New Earth alignment to you?

Ka siu ta siu tai ah.
What memories do you have of The One?

10.
COURSE CORRECTION

MASTERING THE ACT

By my third year in high school, I felt that I had mastered the art of fitting in. This was despite the fact that it felt wrong, and my internal state was one of turmoil. Saying the "right" things, wearing the "right" clothes, hanging out with all the "right" people, and becoming captain and president of all the "right" teams and clubs, I thought I had this gig mastered.

As one did in New England at the time, I found my way into a top liberal arts college and counted down the days until I would be free — just four more years.

What do you do when you feel everything is wrong, yet you try so hard to make it right? In my case, I ignored it, for there was no other way. The beliefs were fixed, anchored in time, and so I felt that four years of college to receive a bachelor's degree was the only way.

I did a great job of pretending I was having fun; all the while, my heart, and my being were suffering in the background, pretending that everything was right when, in fact, it was all wrong. Did I even know that it was wrong? Absolutely not, because I had no frame of reference for following my heart or intuition. I did what I had to do, and that was that.

Perceived mastery over the fitting-in game came to an end once again on July 11, 2000.

COLLISION COURSE

Approximately a month after a group of friends and I took up residence on Martha's Vineyard during our summer break, my entire life came to a halt. I was about to experience the curve ball of all curve balls; I was about to lose my physical form as I knew it, and with that, a whole new chapter would unfold.

Martha's Vineyard is an idyllic New England island off the coast of Cape Cod, where many college students go for the summer to work and feel free. Being a tourist destination for the well-to-do and rich and famous, college students often landed lucrative jobs in the hospitality industry.

When we weren't working, we were making the best of the sun, ocean, and party life.

Two days before life altered course, I had taken a second job as a taxicab driver. These cabs were not your typical cabs. We drove 15-passenger vans, virtually untrained. My dad had insisted that I learn to drive in a Chevrolet Suburban, so the size difference wasn't much, just a few more people along for the ride.

On my first day, I remember standing next to my cab, thinking how great my life was. I was the happiest I had been, possibly ever, and the sense of freedom was invigorating.

The next day, it all changed. I met a 20-year-old man in the office on my second shift. Little did I know at our introduction that he would have a hand in shaping my destiny.

Two hours later, I was on a call to pick up a man and his son from their home and drive them to catch a flight. I parked at the curb in front of the sleepy island airport, and the three of us started unloading their luggage from the back of the van. During this process, the co-worker, with my close friend in the passenger seat, pulled up behind us.

Moments later, I heard the rev of an engine, turned around, and came face to face with the van behind me, going approximately 20 miles per hour. It was here that, unknowingly, the miracles began.

Agony and shock raced through my system as my legs became crushed in between the two bumpers. When the van reversed I fell face-first to the ground, completely conscious and aware of the fact that my legs were unable to move. My entire system stopped functioning other than my mind and vocal patterns as the body directed its energy to prevent blood loss from the leg that had been degloved.

DATE WITH DESTINY

As I was airlifted to a Boston hospital and then throughout surgery, there was a team of angels looking after me, coming to me in my unconscious state and showing me that the course of my life was about to unfold in a different version than how I had planned, for there was work to do they said, and I needed to get on track. I hadn't been listening, and I needed a severe wake-up call to push me into my lane.

They stayed with me the entire time I was unconscious to ensure the transition into my physical body would be one of only gratitude. They encouraged me to fight through the pain and not to give up on myself or the ones around me.

They even arranged for the surgeon who was on duty and the lawyer who drove by the scene of the accident. They set everything up specifically so that I could shift my life onto the trajectory that it was supposed to take. They were with me every step of the way, and for that, I am forever grateful.

They held my hand as I slept, reassuring me that I would be okay. They let me know that this was a temporary moment of discomfort in an otherwise incredible journey. There was nothing to worry about, and no serious harm had occurred. It was a superficial injury, and the functionality of my legs had not been touched. I would learn how to use and appreciate my body. I would not look the same as all the others because I had to know what it felt like to stand out.

As I woke up in the hospital bed after hours of surgery and countless stitches, I was filled with deep gratitude and relief to have two legs. I did not care that one was disfigured because I was overwhelmingly thankful that I still had two.

GRATITUDE'S GIFTS

Everything that could have gone "right" or "wrong" went right. The surgeon who was on duty when I arrived at the hospital happened to be one of the men who had developed the procedure of vacuum-assisted wound healing, which kept me from requiring any additional skin grafts and from suffering infection. He informed me that most people who were in these types of accidents at such speeds would lose at least one leg. Even though one of my legs was degloved and disfigured, I felt only extreme appreciation to still have two.

My appreciation grew when I was told that the boy who was standing next to me at the time of the incident was not harmed. We had split seconds before impact, and I was told that I pushed him out of the way.

His survival was a gift. Angels were sent to ensure that this was only my destiny, not his. His life lessons did not include severe internal injury and probable death. When I later moved to a rehab clinic to finish a second two-week period of recovery, my gratitude only grew, for there were those that I encountered who would never walk again.

And so, this experience became the greatest gift that I could receive, for I only looked at what was "right," and because of this, the gifts kept coming.

DISCARDING FATE

Change in your own life is usually left to fate. This is a concept that says you are not in control of reality and that you lack the ability to create change in your life.

Fate is not a linear concept. Fate is a right of self-determination if you choose to be on the karmic wheel. Fate is a pre-determined meeting point in reality threads if you are not ready to take evolution into your own hands.

Fate is a belief that says you are not powerful enough to embrace each present moment for what it is — a point in time where you have the ability to alter your timeline with your very breath.

When you step off the karmic wheel of fate, you embrace this life for what it is meant to be, an opportunity to evolve into the Source being that you are.

If you have a purpose here on this planet, as many of us do this time around, you will be guided in how to fulfill this, so get ready to walk (or be thrown) into the arms of destiny.

HEEDING THE WHISPERS

If you have a destiny, your Higher Self will orchestrate with the Universe to ensure you are given hints to the direction you are supposed to take to shift onto this track.

If you ignore the hints as they form in whispers, they may present louder and louder until it is a scream that fills the air so that you have no choice but to make the change. Embracing the intense discomfort of conscious course correction prior to the crescendo can save unnecessary heartache, dollars lost, or worse.

I know that it may not be easy; however, when your timing is to shift on course to fulfill your destiny, all else may change. Relationships, situations, and health may crumble, as may the state of the world, from a collective sense.

It is during this change that your ability to direct your mind to look at the positive aspects of the situation will determine the details of the reality that shape you and mankind.

Regardless of when or how you correct course, know that this is your life, your manifest reality, and you have the ability to create great change as your destiny always lies with YOU.

Ai yah, ai yah, ai yah.
Is it time for a course correction, or are you on your optimal track?

11.
THE POWER OF APPRECIATION

HONORING THE INNER KNOWING

Not too long out of the hospital, it was suggested to my father that I required an attorney to ensure all matters were addressed. Worker's compensation was covering the hospital and continued nurses' bills (once at home, there were still dressings to be changed and healing flesh to be tended to), and it was believed there was still a matter of fault to be addressed.

The matter of fault did not sit right with me, and for the first time in my life, I followed my intuition. How could you blame someone for an accident? How could you create more turmoil for someone when there was already enough?

The devastation that held this man and my friend was much worse than what I went through. One believed that he had caused an occurrence in my life that would forever scar me, and the other blamed himself for not stopping it.

At the time, I brought them closer. No blame, no judgment, just love. It was an accident, and to be perfectly honest, I preferred being on my end of the journey as I did not have to get past the guilt.

And so it goes: when the course of one's destiny needs a correction, one will be found. And when one doesn't listen to the signs, they must be made plain as day, so there is no other option.

The reality was that we were all working together. Our Higher Selves in Spirit orchestrating together the gifts that needed to be given.

DIVING INTO DESTINY

The feeling of gratitude continued to pour over me 90% of the time I was in my physical healing process, as my attention and thoughts were beamed in on the fact that I still had two legs that would fully function again.

My healing guides continued to strengthen my field and assisted in turning up the feelings of appreciation so that I could leave behind the track I had been on. I knew that this was a turning point in time and that I was escaping a life that I did not want.

They stayed by my side, day after day, night after night, unbeknownst to me at the time, to ensure my frequency was catching the rays of gold within the situation. They were leaving nothing to chance.

These glimmers of gold were enough to turn events with my attorney into greatness.

When this particular attorney was recommended by my father's friend, no one knew that he also happened to be three hours away from home and driving by the airport on the tiny island of Martha's Vineyard at the exact time I was lying on the ground in devastation with paramedics surrounding me.

When the pieces were put together, we thought it was quite a coincidence. However, this is how destiny unfolds, and there is no such thing as a coincidence.

The Universe orchestrated the circumstances brilliantly, so that even though there was no lawsuit or fault, my attorney was able to unexpectedly secure my get-out-of-jail (corporate life) card through my father's underinsured motor vehicle and business insurance policies.

It was orchestrated perfectly by those who wanted me to get on my path. I thank the Universe and the stars for they all aligned — as they do for each one of us who is ready to embrace their path. When there is destiny at stake, the higher YOU takes no chances. Nothing is left at risk.

Yes, you have free will to see your gifts in every circumstance and to magnify the golden glow within. Yes, you have the opportunity to take lessons and grow, but when it really comes down to it, if you are here for the greater good, the legions have your back, and they will steer you straight if it is absolutely required.

However, you have an abundance of free will to navigate this Earth journey as you choose. You could veer off course altogether and take a different route than the one destiny has laid out. This is the beauty of your free will. You could choose a different timeline, and if your soul agrees, you can interact with this matrix in a completely different fashion.

Destiny, though, seems to be the course of least resistance that will align with your dreams fulfilled.

NAVIGATE YOUR LIFE WITH GRATITUDE

Use the power of appreciation and gratitude to direct the outcome of individual events. We can treat our lives and the experiences we have with extreme gratitude, and the gifts will always be present.

As beings of infinite choice and wisdom, it is only our own conditioned nervous systems and minds that require retraining in order to put us back at the helm of creating reality.

Techniques abound to take back our power on both fronts. It can be kept quite simple — as unwanted thoughts, emotions, and feelings present, we can take care to breathe through them without judgment, bringing rest to struggle. Know that even the most unwanted ones are gifts.

Allow them a pathway to flow back into the central nervous system through the heart's gate, and each individualized point of energy that was disrupting the regulatory flow of body, mind, and Spirit will transform with conscious intent.

USING APPRECIATION TO ACCESS THE VOID

There is a space in between the cells, where all time exists alongside the void. It is the zero-point, where one can harness pure potential energy to drive intent. When we focus our attention on what we are grateful for, the void fills with the most beautiful energy of life.

It is an exquisite golden light that shines into even the darkest corners of despair. It allows heartache to blossom into a rose that, in turn, attracts each and every other wonderment required for you to be the most inspiring, love-filled, and successful version of you possible.

We can use the power of this space to drive a life and a world that we each want to live in by bringing appreciation consciously into our lives. The power of appreciation will bring us each solidly into resonance with New Earth reality planes.

Siu na sia na sia!
How much do you love your life? Can you find reasons to be grateful to be alive?

12.
"DEMOCRACY"

THE INERTIA OF 9/11

On the morning of September 11, 2001, as I observed in a state of bewilderment the first fifteen minutes of the destruction of the World Trade Center, I received the call that catapulted my life into the one that I truly wanted to live.

Due to the inertia of the collective resonance and forces upon the planet, the majority of the world was uniting in a spiral of terror, grief, loss, anger, and hatred. At the same moment, I arrived at a frequency of empowerment and relief due to the result of my inner state of blessings and gratitude over the past year.

To those of you who lost loved ones in those towers, you are honored for your courage, for your ability to weather the storm, and for your bravery in making it through to the other side. Most of you had no choice. Your lives had to go on, for you had families to provide for and loved ones who required your support.

Not only did this rock your entire reality, but many of you also sat there and had the courage to question the truth. Many of you saw through the ruse that was being handed to you by the media and government and had the courage to see through unclouded eyes and question what really happened that day.

However, we are not here to speak about what occurred within the three-dimensional and the debated events of 9/11. We are here to speak of why YOU orchestrated that event.

CREATING A GREATER DIVIDE

Each and every one of YOU who makes up the collective consciousness of the Source of All That Is, why did you, your Selves, orchestrate that fateful day? For YOU did. We all did.

The separation was again broadcast through the airwaves in such dynamism that no one could ignore it, and separate we did. Again, into the chasm of "right" and "wrong": killers and killed, terrorists and heroes, victims and victimizers. Once again, we played right into our trap, the trap that we set up for ourselves so that we could lead each other home.

There is no greater devastation than when mankind is rocked by sudden death and destruction at the hands of murderers, and as time was bringing us closer to the end of illusion, we were required to orchestrate so close to home so that we could see the truth of who we are. But most of us were not awake enough at that time to glimpse the truth.

We sat in the separation and judgment of the situation. Whether you lost a loved one, were one who condemned the "terrorists" or the government and those collecting on the insurance policies, you fell into the hands of separation. As our collective consciousness was not ready for the truth, the separation from that moment only grew.

DISCONTINUING ILLUSION

At that time, as with COVID, some questioned the official story, able to perceive behind the smoke and mirrors, and there were those who were not yet ready to embrace discernment, only able to recognize the official reports.

While the intent of this book is to stir up the energy of love within, there is also an illusion to dissolve.

Before I speak more of what has actually occurred on this Earth plane, I will specifically remind you that this has been set up by YOU, the greatness of YOU, and the Source of All That Is in order to lead you home.

If you have not realized yet, your governments, media, schooling, medical systems, food and water supplies are under the control of the powers that have governed your world for eons. They came here long ago to ensure that they could establish a slave class that would do their bidding. Thus, they could harvest the essential energy streams that were required for their survival.

Many of your human friends have already called them out. Ridiculed they have been, for the time was not yet right for the masses to catch on to the agendas at play. Truth be told, there are species on your planet that do not have your best intentions in mind.

Controlling the essential systems and orchestrating events to create continued separation within the body, mind, spirit complex of the living being perpetuates the fracture of society and divisions within the human frame. Divide and conquer occurs efficiently and broadly.

SILENCED PROTEST

If the human race were to awaken to the truth of this orchestration, there certainly would be a revolt.

Ah, but there has been! But many of you have not been told. In Melbourne, Australia, 300,000 people rallied to protest the lockdowns in which people were kept caged in their homes for almost a year.

How many people did the media report were at these protests? 10,000. A complete media blackout occurred on December 2, 2022, as hundreds of thousands of peaceful protestors made their way from all over Australia to march at the nation's capital. Sources that did report it stated again, 10,000. If you have not yet, please start asking yourself why.

THE STAND

It is the time on the planet for the people to wake up and question their leaders, politicians, and systems of governance and to overthrow the dictators who have taken control of free will, placed it in a dictionary, and made mankind think that they had it under the guise of "democracy."

Democracy has long since died. Our systems were harnessed by the dark forces long ago so that we would remain slaves, and they will continue to do so until we each decide to say, "no more."

Ai ya ku mai ah na, siu ma sia.
Are you ready to take back the helm?

13.
NO MORE

∽o∽

Now, let me please expand here because "no more" has multiple connotations.

REALIZING FRACTALIZED SOURCE

The first significance is based on the fact that you are the Creator. When you know this, you will realize that the war you wage on yourself is manifesting in externalized form.

You are God. You fractured into countless bits of information, including forming different races of species throughout the galaxies, human beings just one of them.

As you differentiated from Source, you began to take on your own identity, visibly removed from the state of love that is the One.

This is your opportunity to say "no more" to the illusion of separation and judgment ways. It is your opportunity to emerge into the larger understanding of holographic reality that you, as an individual, are a reflection of The All, which is an expanded state of unconditional presence and love.

UNMASKING THE LIES

Eons ago, there were not necessarily the control structures that we see in this present moment reality. They have been built over time.

They have been sinking into your skin as you grew in the womb, your physical reality programmed by television and various media outlets, your own internal dialogue and thought processes altered by inter-dimensional inserts that they overlay into your hologram.

This is how they get you — with your complete ignorance. You claim these feelings as your own — *"Oh, I don't feel so good. I'm depressed. I'm suicidal. I'm a worthless junkie. I'm a child abuser."* Whatever the story may be, stop indulging in the warfare that is blanketed upon you. You are the Creator, and your power was purposefully stripped. They robbed you of your knowledge and used your innate abilities against you.

Did you know that your thoughts, behaviors, and actions can be modified at will if you have a certain genetic disposition? If you are still plugged into the false matrix, and even if you aren't but are open to suggestions, they can insert plug-ins into your holographic reality to push you in a certain direction.

I have seen it with my own eyes, experienced it, and witnessed it occur to others. And yet, you continue to think it is you. It is not.

DISSOLVING THE GREATEST ILLUSION

You are the Creator, and it is their God-given duty and right to stop you from acknowledging this.

For this is a game! We together have orchestrated it.

Ka na siu sia tai ah.

The joke is on us. We are playing both sides!

Ka siu tai ah.

Wake up, my friends, and see the truth of this game. Yes, there are two sides, but we designed it. We are the Creator himself.

The only way that we get over the finish line is to recognize this and let go of our need to make the Other wrong and get on with playing the game.

While I tell you this truth on one level, that grave injustices disrupting free will have taken and are continuing to take place, the truth is so much greater — our enemies are our best friends, and these best friends in disguise want us to see the gifts that they provide.

THE NATURE OF THE GAME

Each one of us is playing out a role, a character on a stage in a movie, and projects onto this film strip of life a reflection of what is occurring within the eternal soul. The soul then has the opportunity to take the hero's journey or to come to life from a perspective of revenge – or any modus operandi in between. It is your choice based on the nature of evolution that you orchestrated for yourself before you arrived here this time around.

You then agreed with the other fractalized versions of Source to carry out remembrance processes for each other that came in the form of all sorts of hatred, violence, and disgust.

You recognized the further you came from the truth, the easier it would be to get back. If you hit rock bottom, if you became the violator and the violated, you would be able to easily see that the resistance within was self-perpetrated and that you were doing it to yourself all along.

We designed it as a shock treatment to wake up the essence of the soul. Nothing is so far from the truth; the irony of the situation of separation and dichotomy of the eternal soul would be enough for us to snap out of the stupor and have a big-bellied Buddha laugh at how far we had come.

REMEMBERING THE GAME

As the coming years unfold, many on the planet will begin to awaken to the real gifts of the nature of division.

Here is a suggestion for you — come back to the truth. See yourself for who you are, and as you begin to go through the unraveling of what has been built in society, see those across the lines for who they are, another version of Source. Be willing to embrace the game.

We are here to teach each other compassion and love, but not necessarily by abandoning the sword. We must begin to fight for our right to exist, or the game isn't being played.

Currently, the majority of mankind isn't aware the game is on. Most of mankind is on their knees, having their faces rubbed in the sand by bullies, being kicked over and over in the guts, or being mutilated, raped, and tortured, and they haven't yet learned to say no.

We are coming into an age where the abuse of power ends, yet the version of events that sees this also beholds a mankind that knows how to stand up for one another, other species, and the Earth Mother.

It acknowledges the perpetrator and the abuser as the catalyst for the human race to grow individual and collective boundaries and voices that say, no, we will no longer let you harm.

REVOKING CONSENT

Truly, I write this book to lessen the blow that the coming years will have on the masses of this Earth plane. For the truth will be told, the horrors revealed, and the people will begin to wake. They are already awakening, but not understanding how this could actually happen in society.

We gave permission. Each and every one of us gave permission, and so, quite simply, the answer is plain. All we must do is revoke it.

There is work to be done on the etheric planes as well as the physical. Together, we have made this mess, and now it is time to clean up.

BOUNDARIES

You cannot let them run amuck anymore. The atrocities have been too great, and while they are another version of you, there are boundaries that must be set just as you'd set boundaries for your children and yourself. You ensure that these boundaries keep you and your family safe and on track to live a beautiful life to the best of your ability, and so you must set these boundaries with those reflections of you who are harming others.

And we must do so with love, or we lose ourselves in the process.

Some of you are already on that journey, as I type. Holding the line and doing your duty to fight the evil that reigns on the planet.

But may I ask you how you do this? I know you do this with conviction. I know you do this with a hard-line approach, and so you should. But do you do this with the love of a mother for a child, or do you do this with the rage of a scorned lover?

Many of you are operating from reaction, and I understand why. The terror, the horror, and the atrocities of what one being can do to another are quite evident now, quite black and white, but we must see them in full color.

SEEING THE FULL SPECTRUM

We must see the full spectrum in order to bring about the new era that we wish to see. Many of you out there are holders of the light, bringers of the dawn, and part of the mighty army that is to rise.

However, if you lead from contempt, if you lead from the savage anger or justification that you have used in the past, then you will only be continuing the cycle of revenge.

We must find a new way to deal with injustice, for the breed we call humanity is dying and it will continue to do so unless we shift the trajectory of the momentum on the planet. We must come back to love. Fear has overrun the population, and the frequency is addictive.

RISE IN LOVE

Now, as I write, there has been a reprieve for us to gather our senses one more time. Take this time as an opportunity to enjoy the great beyond but also sharpen your senses for the next round.

How will you do things differently so that you can hold your vortex so cleanly, so clearly, that nothing will shake you?

Can you find the Creator within? When we do this, we find God, and the entire population as a whole shifts. We have a tipping point we must get to on this planet, and I ask those of you who are here for it to rise. Join me on this journey.

But rise not in vengeance. Rise not in war. Rise only in love, and for some of you with certain destinies, this love must be tough.

You will do what is required of you, but ensure it is done with love. You will say "no more," but you will say it from a different space. There is no fear, there is no hatred, there is no anger. There is only justice for the ones who have been left behind, and this justice knows no bounds. It knows only the realms of forgiveness, for it is your duty to reclaim your heart.

Then justice will be had.

Ai ya siu ma sia, ma sia.
It's time for the ending of an era. Will you join the process to dismantle what no longer serves the balance of the whole?

14.
AND SO, IT IS SO

REBALANCING THE ECOSYSTEM

And so, it has been said, the boundaries must be set. When one sees an imbalance within the Self, at some stage, one must address this, or the entire ecosystem of the Self goes out of balance, and disease creeps in.

Consider the human species as one giant version of the Self. We are all fractals of the Source, and we must get our ecosystem in check.

Now, to those of you in your communities, in your families, and those of you in your cycle of personal growth, of course, this comes down to the development of love within your ecosystem, turning away from fear and embracing the Oneness of All That Is. Turn away from contempt and away from your television sets, back to nature, back to the laws of the Universe in which you treat others as you wish to be treated.

To those of you in positions of power on a societal level, I ask you to consider two things.

What would you do if you were in my shoes? Knowing that galactic war is but a moment away from entering this solar system and attacking this planet and this species. What would you do? It is a timeline that has been written, and we must change course.

Think about the calls you are making. Think about the buttons you are pressing. Move away from the eternal need to control and come back to the decisions that will empower this species to not just survive but thrive.

Turn back to the Creator because one day, this will be all over, and the day of judgment comes for each one of us.

JUDGMENT DAY

The day of judgment isn't from an outside occurrence. The day of judgment is from YOU. YOU are the one who decides your fate. YOU are the one who writes your name on the wall.

I am being asked by YOU to remind you of this. You always have free will and you can always make a different decision. You can always go in a different direction, and you can always make amends with the Energy Source of All That Is and your fellow man.

You have a choice. So please do not let these words ring hollow. Seize the opportunity to choose a different timeline, not just for you, but for all of those connected to YOU. Remember, you are a reflection of the entirety of the whole. You are the Creator.

LINING UP

So, what if we choose a different outcome?

Altogether, what if we choose love? What if we choose rehabilitation? What if we choose a planet that thrives in a Golden Age?

The time has returned for Heaven on Earth, and all we must do is line up with the opening.

Ku mai ah, ku mai ah, ku mai ah.
And so it is so, and so it is so, and so it is so.

15.
THE OPENING

MEMORIES RETURN

Lining up with the opening is a feat that is not easily accomplished by the majority of the beings on Earth's surface at the present moment. Due to the afflicted nature of the soul and the evil presence that has dominated the Earth's surface for so long, the memories of the eternal Self have been wiped.

Bit by bit, and then in one fell swoop, they are returning to the people. As above, so below, and as the consciousness of the Eternal Creator opens portal by portal, the doorways to the people's consciousness will also open. One by one, they awaken, and as they do, they require the support, first and foremost, of the Self.

CHAPTER'S CLOSE

How does one know how to support the Self when supporting the Self has not been a tradition throughout the ages of mankind? We have lived through a transactional nature; if I give to you, then you give to me. Quid pro quo. Equal ratios.

It's been the age-old notion of tit-for-tat. It plays out in our personal relationship dynamics, our communities, and our nations. It's an old story, an old ballgame that is nearing its last inning and coming to an end.

No one is the winner, though. No victory is near unless we choose a different course.

Victory does not come with the path that we are on. Victory comes only when the ballgames are put to rest. Opposing sides must find another way to play, choosing instead to rally together.

As we close this chapter on the past, let us look toward our future.

YOUR MOST POWERFUL TOOL

The divide will be bridged; however, it takes the hearts of the masses to line up with the opening.

As we line up with the opening, we must put down the weapons that will otherwise prevent our arrival into this space.

Ah siu ta sia tai ah, ah siu ta sia tai ah, ah siu ta sia.

We must find the opening to the heart.

Bring back your love for yourself, bring back your love for the Others you see, bring back your love for this planet. You have the ability to move time and space with your kindness and your one intent — I come home to my heart.

Our hearts are the most precious tools that we have been gifted in this time/space reality. Truly, the heart's technology is immeasurable. When we surround it with the cloak of darkness, its true powers are suppressed.

BLINDED

This cloak has surrounded mankind for eons. The power struggle has continued for too long. Over and over, the war has raged, and no one has come out the victor. Over and over, we have been taught to fight, kick, and scream, and eventually, they will let us go.

Siu ta sia tai ah.

They have only strengthened their grips.

For when we fight, they fight. When we grip, they grip. When we hold and cling and demand, we find no surrender, and surrender is the gift we must find for ourselves now.

But not the surrender to the alien species that asks for our blood spilled upon this Earth. Be assured they do. They wish for us, as mankind's lifeline, to continue to live within the cloak. Alienated from the truth of existence, alienated from the good that we truly are for each other, and completely ignorant of the impending doom that we bring upon ourselves and each other.

WAR GAMES

Ka na siu ta sia tai ah.

No more. The masses must awaken and realize there is an opening. There is a shred of light to follow — to reawaken the Self into the Oneness of All That Is. This is the complete surrender that I call for.

However, this surrender does not mean there is no fight. At times during the war, surrendering is not the only way. Surrendering is an option. It is an option to find yourself lined up with the opening and on the way back home.

But at times, home must be fought for. It must be treasured enough for the people to say, this is my birthright. This is my design. This is the way that I wish to see the future for myself and my family. I want my children to know the way, the truth, and the light, and I want to be free.

Truth be told, as a society, we require both maneuvers right now.

RISE AND SHINE

How do we find the opening to the heart? This is the age-old question that has been asked for eons. Those who have come before, and no doubt those who come after, will all face a similar peril. How do we evict the demons of the heart space before they take over the entire creationary matrix?

It is quite simple — regain your trust in the Creator, regain your trust in Spirit, regain your trust in the almighty heavens that walk with you day after day after day. Through thick and thin, this God walks with you; this God is YOU, awaiting your arrival. No impatience, no pressure, no demands or requests. Just an unconditional love that, at some stage, when the time is right for you, will show up for YOU.

This is the love that the Creator has for you, YOU have for YOU, and this is the love that we can have for ourselves and others around us. An unconditional presence and acceptance of the Other as the Self will change the world as we know it. It will catapult our awakening to the next stages and guide us through the opening that we are so ready to align with.

My friends, may I share something with you? Your awakening begins now.

Sia na sia, na sia. O nai ah, nai ah.
How will you become the change you wish to see?

16.
HEALING THE HEART

THE HEART EXPLAINED

The heart is a portal of energy that is directly linked to the soul and the universal consciousness of life. It does not exist in every being on this Earth plane. This portal will continue to awaken for all those who are ready to graduate to a nature of peaceful, harmonious existence within themselves and with each other.

We do not necessarily heal the heart overnight. It is a process of evolution that is required to move onto an ascension timeline, which is a timeline in which one transcends the density of the third-dimensional realm and merges with the universal Source light.

The heart's energy field can expand and contract based on the external and internal experiences that one has. The trick to healing the heart and allowing it to blossom into the magnificent generator of energy that it can be is to directly link this portal with the Source.

Linking your heart's portal with the Source can spontaneously occur, especially when magnifying the energy of love and appreciation. The real test that all of us are here to master is the ability to strengthen that link as the world around us, our personal lives, and our relationships come undone.

LOVING UNDER ATTACK

Many moons ago, I made a friend. One who has since turned against me. He waited for me in the depths of the darkness one night and attacked. Where he attacked from, I don't know. All I know was that he was there. And why? I would ask myself that question over and over as my mind wanted to know the answers. However, the mind did not have the answers. The answers would come, though, as Spirit was on the case, on the mission to ensure I knew my divinity.

Under attack, I still loved him. I did not know the separation that was manifest in his own consciousness for him to play the game the way he played.

The way we play the game is the way we see the truth of who we are.

SEPARATION MANIFEST

I was in utero when I saw what happened to my consciousness. I was split from the Essence of All That Is and inhabited a closed mind. It shut instantly, and I lost all sight of myself. In an instant, I knew separation, fear, and pain. This is when my heart's doorway initially closed, rejecting the essence of love because I was programmed in utero that it did not exist.

What I wouldn't do to reverse it. I wish for us all to reverse this pain of separation — to accept it, to love it, to be it, and to be through it because it is time to come to the other side.

CATALYST

The journey of healing the heart escalated for me when the soul, the man I had been unknowingly searching for my entire life, walked up to my door. We met, and chaos erupted. His recognition of my essence set alight the events that unfolded.

I will speak of this in a later writing, as right now, I want to get down to the heart of my awakening.

For now, all I will say is that his arrival on the scene set me free. He set me free, and to do this, he sacrificed life as he knew it, for every bridge burned. Every piece of karma unfolded in front of our eyes. His life burned in flames, and as his life burned, I rose from my own ashes and began to heal my heart.

When one leaves you in the flesh, it is not because they have chosen to. It is because YOU have chosen this pathway as the gateway to your own freedom. The only question is, will you take it?

When I was left due to my own knowledge that he could no longer stay, I experienced the greatest heartbreak that I have ever felt. It was a sense of separation so devastating that not even the Creator himself could take away the pain. It was the pain that he gifted me to walk through so that I could come to the other side.

This was my path. It was to feel devastation, to experience heartbreak, to experience loss — over and over and over in my life so that I could find the truth of this expression and reopen the closed doorway of the heart.

THE UNEXPECTED GIFTS

How do we reawaken the portal that exists within the heart space? First and foremost, we must experience each and every trauma or heartbreak as a gift.

Find the doorway to the heart by saying *thank you for the gift that this experience is giving me*. As you step into the appreciation of each and every moment without blame or judgment, you will recognize the truth of divine orchestration and the nature of the game — that you are on a stage, acting out characters and playing roles to bring each other back to the essence of Self.

Heartbreak from dismantling a relationship is once again a mirror to show you where you decided that you were separate from the Self. You never were, and to fill yourself with the externalized notion that one can complete your own happiness tears you from the value of this individuated journey.

Do not shrink from the pain. Embrace it fully and use this pain as a window into your soul.

CREATING FROM WHOLENESS

Heal the heart first, then from a vibration of the whole, you will find an externalized match. One that will be with you through thick and thin regardless of what plot may play out. They will be in this game with you, and if at some point you must part ways, you will see each other with true eyes of wonderment and appreciation for sharing the journey as you did.

This is the key to truly finding fulfillment in this life. Shift your perspective to one of love for each and every circumstance, and see how your heart flourishes.

INDIVIDUAL BOUNDARIES

Secondly, to find healing of the heart, we must learn how to set boundaries and say no.

Are you willing to be used, abused, judged, lied to, or improperly treated because you do not feel that you deserve better, or have you created a rut with someone in your family or in another life scenario that continues on repeat?

Have you created a life that is inauthentic to who you truly are? Are you continuing the status quo of marriage, friendship, or familial life because you are afraid to rock the boat, or is it easier to continue due to finances or someone who requires your support?

Have you put every single person in your sphere above and over yourself?

The heart's gateway does not just extend externally to take care of others in need. It recognizes that, first and foremost, it must secure its own internal expression of self-care so that the others in your realm have an example of the resonance of self-love.

When you stand up for your personal right to live in an environment that takes care of you and the ones around you, you will know that you are on the way to healing your heart.

COLLECTIVE BOUNDARIES

When you allow abuse into your life, whether that comes in the form of a friend, co-worker, partner, family member, neighbor, world leader, or authoritative body, you suggest that this form of treatment is excusable. No one will win if you do not set boundaries and guidelines of what is acceptable treatment for yourself and your fellow man.

Abuse does not necessarily have to come in the form of physical violence. It also presents in the form of emotional manipulation, domination, or grandstanding that one is better or has power over another. Abuse exerts itself through control.

We are a collective consciousness, and each form of consciousness has an inherent right to exist. However, no one has the right to interfere in the free will and well-being of another.

If you do not stand up for your rights as a self-individuated being, who will?

It is imperative that we learn how to set boundaries for ourselves and those who reside in this dimension along with us so that we can give ourselves and each other the greatest level of care. Allowing the treatment to continue, whether it is from you or toward you, continues the cycle of decay, the decline of the soul, and the splitting from Source.

DRAWING THE LINE

When you say no to perpetrating abuse or when you walk away from misuse of power regardless of who it is from, you say to the universal hologram that you are worthy of more. You are worthy of a life and a world in which respect comes to you. Respect and love co-exist. Without each attribute, the other cannot flourish.

When you begin to set boundaries for your personal world, you will begin to see boundaries take shape in the external nature of your hologram. This occurs in the individual expression at first and will magnify in the external nature of reality.

The one(s) across the divide are here to learn just as much as you are. Setting boundaries is for the evolution of the whole. If you decide to play the role of "victim" this time around, be assured that the Other very much wants to grow out of the frequency of victimizer.

Continuing to be their ally in abuse is detrimental to each of your individualized paths.

THE COLLECTIVE POWER

It is not up to any one of us to make the shift into the externalized Golden Age. It is up to us all. Each one of us has a voice, and when we heal the heart, we are able to express the voice of the individualized and collective psyches in the most effective and transformative ways.

The space to best find the healing of the heart is deeply in the presence of the now. Take the time to address each externalized version of Self that presents to you, regardless of the level of pain. Take a deep breath. Go within. Do not rush any decision, but when you make it, ensure it lines up with the love and golden light that you are.

If you must let go of someone or something, do it with the love of the Creator. There is no judgment, there is no divide, there is only pure grace that knows each of you has co-created the event for each other. Well done.

Typically, we run both patterns of abuser and abused. The abuser in us may present in very subtle ways. Study your patterns of self-care. The abuse of Self can be located here. Dig deep. Don't judge yourself. Focus on becoming more loving to your Self and Others. This is how you find your freedom.

17.
THE PORTAL

WAKING FROM DELUSION

I was once in a daze, a dream of what I thought was reality. In fact, it was a lower vibrational field in which I was trapped. For too long, I stayed, I played, and I endured the hellhole that I had made for myself, or so I thought.

The truth of the matter was that I was finding my way home. Every moment in time that you suffer, you find a way of being that no longer feeds you, that no longer fuels the fire to the eternal expression of the heart. There is never a loss, only a wealth to gain.

Life is only what we continue to believe. The eternal fields of creation are upon you, and you create it however you want.

So today, I say, let us find bliss, let us find hope, and let us find the way home — together.

TOGETHER

This brings me to a place of defining "together." Who is here leading the way? Who is here leading their nations back to their feet once the collapse of all they hold dear occurs? The empires built on greed and corruption will not last, and the balance of nature will be restored.

Those who are uniting to share the message of the true Source and the natural rhythms of the Universe are not limited to their ability to be present in physical form. In fact, they surround us with their wisdom every day. It is up to us whether or not we listen.

WHEN WILL YOU SPEAK?

The ancestors of the lands upon which I have walked lifetime after lifetime have peppered me with questions from the day that I set foot on this Earth plane. When will you speak to the masses? When will you tell them our plight? When will you tell them of our sorrows, our grievances, our ability to hold space, and to be held?

When will you share the message with the world that there is a time coming when they will need our assistance to bring back stability to this Earth plane? When will you tell them of the slaughters, the massacres, the revenge, and shed these occurrences in a different light?

When will you ask them to stand up for themselves and the nations that they represent? When will you tell them that we stand with them? When will you be ready to speak and light the candle for the ones who have passed? And when will you ask them to forgive not only the Self, not only the Other but the One?

When will you speak?

A VOICE FOR THE UNHEARD

My answer has always been vague... until now. I will speak for those who do not have an earthly voice. They stand in these realms of the unseen and wish to give voice to the suffering so that it does not go bypassed, so that it may create a truly lasting effect upon the nations that stand here now, knowing not which direction to choose.

The ones on the ancient lands who held the Earth tribes in balance and harmony have gone unrecognized by the majority of society. Their lineages are out of reach for many, but the ancient imprints still run in your DNA regardless of what race or nation you associate with today.

You need not be Black to know the plight of those who suffered apartheid in South Africa.

You need not be Indigenous to know the devastation that the chains and stolen generations had upon the people of the Australian lands.

You need not be Native American to feel the bloodshed that was endured.

You need not be Tibetan to feel the corruption of the empire and those who sought to gain control of sacred land.

Yet these people, like many others, have felt unheard, unseen, and abandoned by the greater collective that has left their plight to that of a minority race without recognizing the greater picture of the whole.

Their injustices have been yours as well, and without recognizing the greatest threat to mankind, you continue to perpetuate the very cause of their attempted genocide.

That is, you continue to promote separation by implying that, because of their perceived bloodline and color, they are not your brother or sister; thus, they are not those for whom you stand.

REAWAKENING TO THE STARS

The species of mankind is not alone in their journey to the stars. Many other races of galactic species exist beyond the borders of our solar system and within them as well.

When you recognize your own species as your blood despite the color of your skin, the texture of your hair, or the language you speak, then you will be on your way to incorporation within galactic society as a whole. Only then will you be ready to know the infinite nature of the Universe.

Until that time, we continue the work here on the Earth plane, for here is where we find the resurrection of The One.

Siu na sia, na sia.
Let the nations unite in song.

18.
TIMING FORETOLD

TIMING DIVINE

This leads us to a chapter regarding timing, as our own time has come as a species to restore the Golden Era of our hearts and our souls.

We do this together, as it is a reawakening of many hearts that will put an end to tyranny on this Earth plane, but it is, of course, a journey of the individual. And so, as you walk your own path, allow your own journey's divine timing to manifest in perfection.

Divine timing is something that is self-created. It is an individual construct. This timing rests within and manifests externally. Your ability to line up with this universal flow will show your mastery of the divine.

TIME LOOPS

As you awaken to the fact that we do not live in a linear reality, but experience time loops based on choices made, you can find your way out of karmic patterns and onto an intended path — whether that is one that you laid down before you incarnated this cycle, or whether it is a path that you want to boldly and bravely create by denying destiny and starting again.

Walking out of time loops requires an awareness on the nature of divinity and presence.

DIVINITY DEFINED

Everything in this Universe is divine. Divinity is the entirety of this Creationary matrix and does not differentiate light from dark. The power forces that held our planet and people have operated from this truth, knowing that divinity was them, and ensuring that you believed otherwise, not only through religion but also through certain teachings of the New Age.

They recognized that divinity was always at work and used this universal power to accomplish their own means. This, too, is perfectly divine.

When relating to divinity, the most helpful construct is to recognize that divinity is The All. When you line up with the timing of your soul's heartbeat, you are working in perfect rhythm and harmony with divine nature and the Universal Law of One.

COORDINATING DIVINITY

Each and every moment contains the present. Each and every moment contains a gift. When we line up with the universal force that is dictating the present trajectory, then we coordinate our divine timing. This is easiest done in what Eckhart Tolle refers to as the "now."

Here, we find the path of least resistance, and we can tune into the subtleties of divine order. There may be a flow of energy to be at a certain place at a certain time, or the divine timing may call for the release of a person, situation, or emotion.

You tap into the flow of this universal order by recognizing the energy of the present moment and responding in kind with a vibrational answer to this energy rather than ignoring or resisting it.

At times, we may choose to force, and all we must do is let go. Surrender to the present moment and line up with the events as they unfold with a vibrational match that most likely will include some form of action.

ACTION + TIMING = RESULT

All actions lead to results. However, when we start to line up our actions with the timing of the present moment, we begin to master our own destiny — individually and as a collective species.

A dear friend introduced to me the phrase, "right action, right timing."

This is all you require to manifest phenomenal results. There is no effort in this; it is a space of synchronicity with The One.

MASTERING MANIFESTATION

The question for many is, how do you truly let go of control in a reality field where you must master the process of conscious manifestation to bring about the results that you wish to see?

Because the universal flow of energy will present differently for each one of us on this Earth plane, it is up to our own soul's evolutionary process and the choices that we make as to when our timing synchronizes with the destiny of our soul.

Mastering the process of manifesting a New Earth timeline requires you, at some stage, to heal the resonant frequencies of lack and separation within your own Self. As you do this, you begin to resonate with self-worth and the love that you are destined for. If we continue to manifest from our wounded reality, we will continue the karmic cycle until we are able to leap out.

Timing, though, is not linear. You can decide to have a jump in perspective, experience, and cellular state at any moment. This thought alone will change the trajectory of your soul.

Processes are abundant in how to master your reality; however, the first and foremost port of call would be to restructure outdated and limiting beliefs.

All in all, your timing is up to you. You can push against the universal call of your soul, or you can give in to the beauty that it has to offer you regardless of what feeling or circumstance the moment presents.

As you each line up with your individual call to heal the heart, the synchronicity of the Universe will begin to pull more and more into a timeline that supports the creation of systems and synchronicities that create an environment on Earth of peace and resilience.

Ah sia, siu ma sia.
Know that all is well.

19.
FORGIVE THEM

∽о∽

REBELLION

It is the timing for the masses to awaken and to rebel against the forces of control that have been at the forefront of reality for too long. The masses will see what has been done and want their revenge.

Please hear this — revenge is not the way. It is not the way to awaken hearts, and it is not the way to free souls.

The true freedom comes in the awakening of the portal that is the heart.

QUESTIONS

I have three questions for you:

What will it take for you to awaken your heart?

What will it take for you to see the everlasting truth of the situation in front of us?

What will it take for you to see that there is no divide, there is no separation, there is no truth other than the truth that we are each a fraction of the whole?

In this truth, our brothers and sisters that you think have done you wrong truly have not.

They have only been there as a gateway to your awakening, a gateway for your own process to reclaim your heart.

THEY KNOW NOT WHAT THEY DO

Forgive them, not for what they do, but for that they know not what they do. If they truly knew what they did, they would not be able to stand in front of you and speak another day. Their eternal Selves would be busting through the front lines to ensure that they put a halt to their actions and the situation long before now.

However, the shroud that has covered mankind has been thick, and the masses could not see the truth of the existence of the eternal flame within. They could only see through the lens of separation — you and me.

So, forgive them not for what they do; forgive them, for they know not what they do.

TURN WITHIN

The veil is thinning. Soon, you will see you for YOU, and you may not know which way to turn, and the pain and the regret may be too much to withstand.

The only way to turn is back within. You will not be able to blame an outside source without catastrophic results for yourself. When one looks outside for his sense of relief, understanding, judgment, manipulation, or blame, the only one who suffers is the one who perpetrates the guise of separation.

And for you, I want so much more. For my family, my tribe, and my fellow brothers and sisters, it is time to reclaim the understanding that we are whole. We are already whole, and no more blame can be placed.

When you awaken, you must take the blame and transform it into something much greater. You must find it within yourself to restore your own heart and forgive.

Forgiveness is not something that solely comes from the outside in. To truly forgive, we must go from the inside out. Within is where the heart lies, and this is the gateway to the true expansion of mankind.

We look outside to fix the planet, to fix problems, and to find a cause when truly it is only the eternal essence of the Self that is the gateway home.

Ai ya, siu mai ya siu tai ah.
Are you ready to see through the eyes of One?

20.
SELF-DELIVERANCE

BETRAYAL

I will tell you a story of enormous proportions, for until it occurred, I did not know what forgiveness truly was. Within the past three years, I created by default two situations in which I felt betrayed, used, abused, put to shame, and misheard. Past programming and unseen shadows were still surfacing in my creations.

These situations did not occur because of outside circumstances; no, in fact, they were exact representations of what was occurring within my heart. It was fractured, for it still saw separation from others.

Agreements were made with bonds in place, yet when it came time to dissolve these two separate relationships, I did not listen to the timing. I continued ahead, not wanting to shatter the status quo. I was content and unable to reconcile that the timing of the moment called for us to walk our separate ways, though the insights were overwhelmingly loud and clear.

So, when betrayal occurred in both instances, I did not know what to do. I struggled against the fact that one could treat others like this. I used the guise of non-communication to justify why there was a breakdown in both friendships, when really all that was occurring was a mirror being held to my own heart so that I could see the truth of what still required repair.

Over and over and over again, the same message appeared.

"Listen to the timing, Zhara. Attach to no one, attach to nothing. Allow God to work through you, for you are but an instrument of the Creator in this lifetime and if you won't stay on your track, we will be forced to intervene." And with the assistance from my non-incarnate team, each and every moment has shifted into an incredible gift.

SOUL SEARCHING

Our timelines are not fixed, and every lump of coal can be but a diamond.

Knowing that we can make any situation turn into the greatest gift that has ever been given, I will speak to you about forgiveness as I have experienced it. It is not the Other that we must forgive; it is the Self.

The two times my human ego decided to turn separation into a battle of justice, I asked Source to show me what I needed to see.

What was it that I was missing, to encounter these storms again? Why did I need to see separation through a lens that was most uncomfortable, in which I experienced abuse, misuse, and abandonment, and then reacted by deflecting back the energy of the Other in the form of a verbal altercation?

The answers lay within.

The forgiveness of the Other I could easily accomplish. I could see very clearly the inner trauma at play, and respected that we were each present to deliver the gift of insight if we chose to take it.

In one situation, I could see the fire and steam pointed at me. I could forgive this aspect of the Other that required the use of blame and judgment to cover the deep pain within.

I could see this, but why couldn't I find freedom within? What was it that would set me free from repeating this cycle in which I loved another and lost?

The separation I was shown was not with the Other. It never had been; it never would be. It was always within the Self.

ALCHEMY

For this reason, the only clearing that would take the unrequited love that I had for each of these friends and alchemize the pain into the gift of gold was forgiveness for abandoning my essence of Self and pretending that an outside source had power over me.

Dropping all pretense that I was not responsible for each circumstance as it unfolded took away any discomfort because I experienced the truth that there was only me. This is my reality field, and if I take responsibility for it, I can create a different outcome.

Each experience was a beautiful gift in which the palpable energy current of forgiveness washed through the physical body, and the stagnant remnants of the circumstances dissolved in an instant.

There was no more pain, judgment, or discomfort to the energetic systems of physicality. The truth was just there, so loud and clear, so beautiful and light that shards of pain were replaced with unconditional love for the Other.

GOLDEN GRIEF

The potency of love available for each one of us is unquantifiable. Yet as I write, I feel a penetrating heartache for the people who have not yet found the ability to free the Self of the misery that still entraps them.

Yes, they have glimpses of love, I know. They have understanding, but do they know the true gift that is awaiting them? They do not, and still I do not, for I have been indoctrinated within the shallow halls of humanity's crises as well. The more that I step into the arms of bliss, the more I am reminded that the fractalized Others have yet to come to their truth.

I cry for the pain of the truth hidden; it hurts me to the depth of my core because I want the people to remember. I would move mountains for the blessings that are here for them; right here, right now, they are so exquisite, so golden, and filled with light beyond what they can possibly imagine; they will wonder why they ever lived in silence and sleep.

And so, I cry, not knowing how to awaken them, not knowing how to remind them, not knowing how to ensure that the work I am here to do is done. And yet, I am also free, knowing that the depths of pain that I experience along with the Others will end in a shattering of the chains that hold mankind, and the heartbreak will be no more.

LOVE AWAITS

The masses will awaken, and when they do, they will have the opportunity to return to their truth. Love will be waiting, the truth of the eternal existence of the Self will be present, and it will be only their choice that separates them from the greatest blessings that mankind has ever seen.

It truly is a choice. We can choose to live in a world of suffering, or we can choose to escape from the shadows. We have this ability to affect matter in a way that is only beginning to come to mankind's awareness, for the darkness has had its hold on our independence. However, we are awakening as a species.

It is time for the rebirth of mankind's future. It begins with a choice to recognize the power that you hold as the eternal essence of Source. If you are willing to see the chasms as only opportunities for self-deliverance, you are on track to opening your heart.

TO RISE OR FALL?

So, I ask you, especially YOU, who sits with the opportunity to affect great change, what will you choose?

Will you assist in the greatest awakening that mankind has ever seen, or will you sit on the sidelines?

Recognize, though, the sidelines are no longer there, and if you choose this position, you will fall. It is time to rise or fall back, and if you choose to fall back, know that at any time, you can rise up.

Siu nai ah na, siu nai ah.
Find your grace, find your expansion, and be the love and free being that you were born to be.

21.
COMING INTO OUR OWN

∽∾∽

TRANSMUTATION POINT

The Great Awakening begins, but what does that look like for our current modern-day society? You see factions, divisions, right/wrong, us/them, and this is exactly the state that has put us here in the first place. These chasms will grow and grow until the people have had enough of the torture and the pain, and then they will see the truth for what it is — those they condemn are just another version of the eternal Self.

When enough of us become this critical mass, the transmutation point will have been hit, and the coming of the Golden Age will be heralded. But is this a timeline set in stone for everyone? It is not. It is only a timeline for those who desire to go down the path of least resistance, to shed the egoic nature of the Self and see through eyes reborn.

CHOICE

We all choose our own points in time to remember that we are fractalized versions of the One. As we draw nearer to the Golden Age, I ask that you choose your points of resonance.

Where are you going? What do you want to see? Where is our society headed?

Is it headed for destruction or for the greatest gift that mankind has ever seen?

THRIVING THROUGH THE STORM

No matter what you see take place in this reality field, please hold to the fact that what is occurring is of an alchemical nature, and we must hold fast to the mast as we make our way through the storm. So, I only see these facets of breakdown as great gifts. Watch the unraveling of society as we know it and show only appreciation for what will occur.

Trust the eternal essence of God in this process, for it is a process that will happen with or without our conscious consent, and the most helpful thing that we can do is get on the path of least resistance.

Find your breaking point and go further. Show the world what you're made of and do what you came to do, for you came to do something with your time on planet Earth. You did not come to sit as an observer. You came to get involved.

YOUR POSITION

Many of you were specifically planted in positions of power for this great unfolding.

What path will you choose from where you sit?

Each and every one of you has the opportunity to bring great light to the world, to undo what has been done, and to wish well-being for the others within your realm.

You have the opportunity to create a change, to create a movement like never before. Will you ride the wave?

THE TIMING IS NOW

This moment in time is unlike any other. As the masses rise, so does the groundswell that includes each and every one of us. Together, we form a wave — an ocean, in fact — for the truth of this human existence is that we are a droplet in the great, big, fractalized sea.

THE POWER OF THE SEA

You are a cluster of walking water molecules, as are your colleagues, your friends, your family, and this very large faction of mankind.

What happens when water molecules combine en masse? Well, that depends on the intention given, doesn't it? Sometimes, the sea will rage; sometimes, it will deliver gentle laps on the beach. Sometimes, there will be a trickle, and other times, a tidal wave.

The water molecules together create the destined events of time. They together control the outcome of the population. And so, keep this in mind as you journey together. You are but a fractalized droplet of the sea; however, en masse, you create a wave, a storm, a safe haven, a blueprint for a new destiny.

You get to choose.

Kai ah, kai ah, kai ah.
The water is awakening.

22.
MANKIND'S BLUEPRINT

THE TEMPLATE

And so, it came to pass that at the beginning of time, we, together as the essence of All That Is, created a template for mankind to thrive. A blueprint, if you will, that was handed to every man, woman, and child as they entered this existence. This template was their birthright.

When they each arrived in this Universe, into the densities that make up our solid world, the templates cracked and were distorted by the stress that the population was under. This distortion is currently under repair, and many of the human race will be able to restore their original coding within this physical matrix.

It is a destined event to ensure that the human population comes back up to speed, back in line with the Creator. However, if one does not know that this template exists, then how does one find a foothold to restore it?

Luckily, it is not happening by chance. The upgrades are coming for us at light speed as we hang on for the ride. However, there are ascension symptoms that come along with the journey, and there are ways to fast-track and support the process. Suggestions can be found at the end of the book.

For now, let's look at the original template destined for mankind.

THE HOLY GRAIL

There was once a time when the population of this planet thrived. It was a time when there were no enemies. There was no war, and there was only a distinguished peace and air of calm.

Joy reigned, and the people were the incarnation of their birthrights. The time is upon us to restore this Holy Grail to the people of this land.

The Holy Grail lies within the eternal waters of the Self and is the imprint of the soul upon the physical time/space matrix. In other words, the chalice that generations have been told to seek is none other than you.

TRANSITION PROCESS

Many of us hold the keys and codes to this unfolding. I write this book specifically to locate the ones of us who are here to do this work.

Many of you already know; some of you are just waking up, and a few of you are already on the tracks you originally laid for your destiny path. But the tracks are much bigger than we could possibly have imagined, for the groundswell is coming, and we must be ready.

There are those out there who have received and are receiving similar transmissions to the ones here. The transmission states that there is a certain order that is to be returned to mankind and the planetary grids in order for us to fulfill the destiny of the "promised land."

There is a transition process, and the transition process must begin now, more earnestly than what has previously been feasible.

DECENTRALIZED COMMUNITIES

As we navigate back to the beacon of the heart, we can begin to align small-scale decentralized communities located at very specific points on the Earth's grids. These energy centers will be sheltered from the coming storms, and the structures and resonances that you require will be gifted to you as you begin your work.

FREE ENERGY

There are many beings with free energy technologies that will bring you gifts behind closed doors. The ones that ask for your submission in some form or another would be better off declined. No longer can you work with control or power over models, as they will be destined to fail. As systems crumble, you must rely on your own ingenuity to rebuild.

The hidden geniuses are among you, and many will step to the forefront to offer their gifts as you go through the planetary rebirth. As you choose who to work with, you must find the resonance of the heart.

Greed, profit, and unscrupulous motives are the beginning of a long, slippery slope, and those who have the betterment of mankind naturally at the forefront will be greatly rewarded many times over.

These people will have their hearts intact. They will know that they are The One, perhaps not in intellect, but the resonance in their cellular structure will be true. They will come with open arms and will not deceive. You will feel their joy from a mile away and know that the heart's portal is in the lead.

They will give you access to free energy and know how to do so with a very basic procedure involving sound and light.

It will not involve small-scale generators or need to be accessed through technological advancement. The real technology is stored within your DNA, and they will teach you how to commune with nature and the wisdom of your cells in order to reactivate it.

The energy center of your mitochondria holds more energy than just the energy that is required to drive the physical form. Your mitochondria are storehouses of energy, and that energy can be redirected to the physical plane.

ACCESSING SOURCE LIGHT

However, you will be tested before you are allowed to access this potential. Your heart must be in line with the people. It must be in line with basic goodness and a love that treats everyone in front of him or her as the king or queen they rightfully are.

They each hold the keys to their own kingdom.

When we are ready to look outside of illusion and turn current society on its head, looking for value from the inside out and not just the outside in, we as a society will be ready for the gifts this free energy brings.

Until the time that you are able to access the true wealth within, use what is required to create an enhanced civilization, but know that if you look externally, you will miss the real fire that burns.

CULTIVATE DISCERNMENT

Two words of wisdom and also of warning — cultivate discernment. Everyone who comes forth may not be of pure intent. You may feel the nudge of intuition telling you that you should steer clear. Do so without hesitation and judgment.

It's important to know that there are various agendas at work, and different alien factions are behind a great deal of the manipulation of many well-intentioned individuals and organizations on the Earth plane. Do not walk in fear, but walk with eyes wide open that are able to distinguish truth from fiction. For many of us, we cultivate the wisdom of discernment through trial and error. This is how we grow.

Know that when you do find an edge that is grating, you are allowed to step back. You have made no commitments to anyone other than the eternal Self, and in committing to your Self, you commit to the whole. If there is a time to retreat, do so unapologetically but with kindness and humility. You always have the right to say no.

EVOLVING DNA THROUGH WATER

As we move forward in establishing a new baseline for society, there will be those of you who have been gifted financial measures and accumulated resources in this lifetime, and you will wake up to the fact that these are not resources solely for your own self-pleasures. Have you considered funding experiments in upgrading human DNA?

I am not speaking from within the science laboratory, although this too is a possibility. I point specifically to upgrading the water systems of this planet, for the water systems are the purification mechanisms of the human soul.

Ai ya, ku nai ah na, sia tai ah.
It's time for the rebirth.

23.
WITHIN THE WATER

Water is the birthplace of creation, but it has been misguided, misused, and misunderstood specifically because the truth of its real nature will set the people free.

It is the Creator, the created, and the entire essence of Source as One. It houses the energy streams of thoughts, emotions, manipulations, devastations, genetic alterations, genocides, creative bursts of genius, but first and foremost, the Source of love.

Water holds the imprints of The All. As we reconnect with her, we bridge the gap between destiny foretold and destiny unfolding.

MANIPULATION OF THE GENES

When those in power decided they had to maintain their power, they looked at how a population could be controlled. Slavery was the obvious answer, but how do you keep a population enslaved, keep them working for you, and keep them moderately content while they are doing so? If they are too happy, they find the keys to the kingdom. If they are in overarching despair, the clock doesn't tick, and if they are awake to the fact that they are slaves, they will, at one stage or another, revolt.

So, they tampered with the system that would most widely be used, and with this tampering, they knew they had an ace up their sleeves. They hit the water supplies hard.

THE BIRTHPLACE OF CREATION

Water is the birthplace of creation. It is the living womb space in which our cells reside. Our very essence, our very fabric that makes us man or woman, sits within the water molecule.

Now, that may sound odd to some, as from any logical standpoint, we appear as flesh and bones that is solid in structure, and that we are. However, water is our driving force, our driving makeup within the human genome, and also the driving force within human expression.

ELECTRICAL POTENTIAL

The body is an electrical system capable of recharging its own batteries and running an organized and centralized current of electromagnetic energy through waveforms that manifest in a conductor of water.

What is the charge of electricity that your form is able to hold?

Due to the powers that have been on the planet, if you drink ordinary water from taps, filters, bottles, and even from the majority of springs, not only will you be ingesting varying degrees of toxic dissolved solids that shut down your body's internal brilliance and alter the chemical makeup of your naturally designed system, you will also be devoid of the minerals that contain the answers to life. The water that makes up your genetic material will be bleak, and conductivity will be far, far less than optimal, or virtually non-existent.

It is a trick as old as time — hold them back from their original make-up, and you hold them back from their original destiny.

And so, the story has gone. Without the electromagnetic charge surging through the powerhouses of the body's physicality, the body's physicality stays daftly ignorant of its true capabilities. With its charge weak, the body is unable to sustain itself or the current from which all life flows.

RESTORING THE CHARGE

The true power of the living being contained everything within; not one thing required altering in the physical form. The body knew how to do what it was capable of: sustaining life.

Bring in the medical systems and the control structures that said health was outside of you. Chaos ensued, not only in the physicality, but in society as a whole. We must find the answers to these breakdowns, not outside, but within.

The most immediate way to find the true power within the Self is to return it to its natural state. The quickest way to alter this on the level of physicality is through the body of water in which YOU live.

BOLD RESEARCH

When you begin to look at the research conducted on the water molecule over the past century, you begin to put together the pieces of a puzzle that will together redefine how we treat our planetary and individual bodies of water.

Mu Shik Jhon, Albert Szent-Gyorgyi, Dr. Gerald Pollack, Dr. Masaru Emoto, Veda Austin, Mae-Wan Ho, and Rudolph Steiner are only a handful of the leading-edge researchers and quantum thinkers who have presented significant glimpses into the gene pool's relationship with this flow-filled medium.

Structure, coherence, and the ability of water to magnify light are all critical factors in restoring the health, vitality, and innate ability of the water molecule to nurture people and planet.

Emoto and Austin are two of many who have clearly demonstrated the vast storage capacity of the water molecule and that the infinite field of intelligence that passes through an individuated person's lens can manifest in water.

Their experiments reveal that the innate consciousness of water can construct a living replica of the waveform of energy that is broadcast through emotion, sound, and intent.

The aforementioned researchers together demonstrate what scriptures and indigenous tribes have been saying all along. Our waters are holy.

THE POWER OF INTENT

Their scientific work brings us clues as to how we can rapidly move from old world to New Earth. The Creator has encoded the living being with an ability to focus the power of their intent into every living molecule on this planet.

The experiments with water and intent are alive and well. The emotional charges will show up in the water — most of the time. Depending on the intensity of your intent, and the ability of your mind and cellular structure to hold a belief, the mind will encode the matrix of the water molecules.

If one's intent is powerful enough to shift time and space, it can show up very clearly in the water molecules. Emoto began this research with the frequencies of emotions and words, and Austin picked up where he left off by demonstrating how water molecules change form based on the information they are imprinted with.

They prove that sound and light will alter the structure of water. Place an object next to a petri dish of water and watch the water within the petri dish mimic the shape of the object. Yes, this is occurring, but why? Is it just the power of intent to grab hold of a concept and make it true? Or is there another universal truth at work?

INTENDING HEAVEN ON EARTH

We affect time and space so clearly with our intent. It is always our intent. It has always been our intent. It will always be our intent. Do we want the water molecules to appear as a gigantic ladder climbing their way to heaven? How can we harness the power of our intent and use our abilities for what is actually required right here, right now?

What if we joined our water molecules together and used this God-given ability to create Heaven on Earth? Climbing the ladder together, out of the petri dish, into real-world scenarios. It can and will be done.

When enough of us hold the vision for peace, love, and harmony within the cells of our bodies and vibrate cleanly at this resonance, we will create a magnificent transformation in our physical world.

Each body of water going on this ride of fifth-dimensional ascension must be addressed. It does not happen overnight, and it does not happen with only a finite amount of people involved.

We must ensure the baseline of consciousness is transformed within mankind. When the critical mass is achieved, the bodies of water with the ascension timeline already encoded will transmit a new frequency to the remaining souls who are here for a similar journey. This transmission will be delivered through the electrical systems that run through their physicalities and their souls.

COMMUNICATION STREAMS

Simply stated, these physicalities are water, and these souls are housed in water.

From the very beginning of time, water was used as a storage house for information, and it contains the entire history of mankind, not only in the DNA fragments that have yet to be reactivated in many, but also in our planetary sources.

The planetary sources are awaiting the wake-up call from the essence of Self. The more beings that consciously bless the waters of the Earth plane, the faster the heart activations transmit to the people.

Everything on this Earth has a resonance. Water itself maintains its own resonance through its Source. However, due to the alterations of the Earth's grids, it, too, disconnected from its eternal Self.

As we recognize the power of the Earth's streams, rivers, and oceans to direct energy currents to different grid points on the planet, we'll begin to see the Earth is also going through a process of remembering her own Self.

As she strengthens, we strengthen, and as we strengthen, so does she.

FIRST PORT(AL) OF CALL

Earth and mankind are ascending frequency together. Each is made primarily of water, and this is the first and foremost access point for us to create change.

Let's open our eyes even wider to what is possible to transmit through this primal medium.

The living waters within are the rivers of energy that run through time and space to connect your original essence as The One to your current time/space location as a manifest being. These currents also connect you with your other aspects of Self that did not fractalize into density.

The grounding of these living waters into third-dimensional form are our mechanism to restoring the Source's grace in our externalized world. Generating the frequency of love from the heart's portal into the waters housed within our physicalities and the Earth brings forth the current of grace to the waters in manifest form. When the living waters internal are merged with the waters of the physical plane, they bridge the divide that erupted when we split as The One.

Water in waveform transmits information beyond time and space. It alters the nature of reality and is also reality. It acts as a quantum transmitter and a quantum receiver and contains the entire quantum soup of Universal knowledge. It contains every bit of knowledge that is manifest in you and is also you. You are particles and light, just like water. And you, as an individual or as a collective, can move as a waveform into the reality field of your choosing.

New Earth, anyone?

CHOOSING FROM THE HEART

Activating the heart's portal in conjunction with the understanding of water's innate gifts allows you to connect with the timelines that your heart desires.

The higher heart sits within a frequency band invisible to the untrained eye. However, it intersects at the point where your physical heart resides.

The bandwidths of your higher heart and physical heart overlap and together create the resonant frequency of your life.

What frequency is pumping through your blood? What is transmitting information to your soul? Turn off your televisions and media that have been very purposefully designed to pump fear into your internal waters and take yourself into the natural world.

Bathe in the creeks, streams, and oceans that were designed to nourish your soul and are able to cleanse your internal rivers from the electromagnetic smog that blankets the Earth and etheric planes.

As you visit these natural wonders, recognize that they store consciousness and memories of every bit of Earth's existence, including the slaughters, devastations, and wars. However, because water will mirror your intent, each molecule holds the gold standard for cleansing and purification as well.

Which frequency will you amplify, and which ones will you cleanse?

A NEW STANDARD

As you feed yourself, take care to nourish with revitalized, remineralized, and blessed waters that were destined to care for your being and your soul.

Ditch the tap water as it has been polluted beyond recognition and contains every element from neurotoxins and carcinogens in the form of fluoride and chlorine, to endocrine disrupters that are altering the natural balance of your internal world.

Yes, you have the innate capability to bless water and transform it into the most beautiful crystalline structure available to mankind while transmuting all resonant frequencies of contaminants within, but are you equipped for that journey?

Have you merged with your soul and the Source of all that is? Is your belief up to speed with the power of the Self, and is your electrical system able to generate the energy required to move density?

If the answer is not quite yet, then take measures to ensure that what you are encoding your body with is of purity, love, and best intentions. Doing this will assist you in embodying the Creator that you are.

Ah siu na sia, ku mai ah.
The waters within open to eternal life.

See Appendix at the end of the book for suggestions to upgrade water.

24.
SOCIETAL EVOLUTION

WILL YOU LEAD?

And so, the human blueprint evolves, but what of this society that we must reframe? What of this society that calls for a complete overhaul? You see it happening in front of your faces. There is no more room for the faint of heart. Those who cannot see the eternal essence of the Self will no longer have control over the populations, and as their numbers decrease, there must be those who are ready to stand in their hearts and lead.

Is that you? Are you receiving the call to step to the forefront and lead your people home? The masses will be awaiting you. They will be waiting for you to give them direction, to tell them what to do, where to go, as there will be no food, no shelter, nowhere to turn as it all unhinges. In the coming days, months, and years, we must make ready the systems that are required to transition from the old to the new.

STATUTES FOR THE SOUL

These systems are ones in which every being is cared for on this planet regardless of race, socio-political affiliation, religion, or social status. They are ones in which abundance reigns for the whole, regardless of one's ability to accumulate wealth. It is one in which basic needs are met, not by a governmental body that exudes control, but by a growing allegiance of the people for the people.

This is the destiny of mankind — to take care of its own.

DISTRIBUTION OF WEALTH

There are those of you who have walked this Earth destined for wealth. Destined to be the divine blueprint for the accumulation of material resources, and many of you who have this blueprint were put here specifically at this time to assist those without wealth.

It does not mean you give up your financial liberties so that you yourself lose what you have acquired. You are here to distribute resources that you discern in alignment with your Highest Aspect of Self as well as to teach the people how to accumulate wealth in their own right.

Disseminating this information is required to turn a society of poverty and system-stricken individuals into wealth generators. These necessary tools for thriving can be embedded into New Earth educational sectors that aim to develop the innate potential of the living being.

HEALTH CARE

The systems that have been shown to many of us who are tapped into the New Earth template are specifically designed to ensure that the masses have true health care outside of the medical and pharmaceutical systems, regardless of what they are able to afford. It allows for the truth of the people to be known — that they are cared for at all times, regardless of what their material status holds.

The people must be cared for. It is our right and responsibility as self-individuated beings to insist that this occurs. We cannot watch another needlessly die when we actually have the power to affect this change on a systemic level.

When a man walks by another in their time of need, we only walk by our own Self. How do we make this transition to one of love, care, and peace for all?

ECONOMIC REFORM

It is time for fundamental change, to rewrite the codes of our economic systems to come from a place of love and liberty for all. To come from a space of, "I have enough, so I help you with what you require." When you understand the infinite abundance that you harness by helping a reflection of yourself, it is easy to say, "I know that you are a reflection of me, and so I will give you what I need."

I need a home, I need a refuge, I need a safe space to be. If that is the reflection I see in you, I look internally within me, but I also help you. This is the power that we have for each other.

It does not come from a space of need or from greed but from a space of true care and consideration for our extended family, knowing that as we help those around us, we will, in turn, be cared for.

There is a time in our life when we are all in need of a leg up, a shoulder to turn to, a hand to hold, and it must first begin with how we write our societal statutes.

How can we invest in each other? How can we ensure we are all cared for? Remember, we are caring for the Self. The eternal nature of creation is one of reflection, and these images you see in your hologram, these other people, are you staring back at yourself.

CARING FOR THE CARERS

It is time to take back our destiny and care for those who care for others. Many practitioners and facilitators have the ability to assist in well-being and the return to holistic health, including using their healing hands. Most practitioners choose to set their services at prices that a large population cannot afford as they too, have bills to pay and mouths to feed.

The way of our ancestors was to provide for the providers. The circle was of One, and it worked. Everyone was cared for, and health was not dictated by whether you had financial means. It was dictated by the choice of whether the soul wanted to stay or go. Now, the soul is pushed into a corner and lives in a fight or flight state due to whether it can outrun the measures that have been inflicted upon society.

We, as a galactic and global society who have the hearts of mankind in mind, aim to return the people to their full state of glory, not just in hearts, health, and well-being, but with a system that intrinsically cares for the whole. It is not just a society with huge hearts that will assist in paving the foundations for the Golden Age; it is the practical application of those hearts.

Ai ya na ku nai ah.
Is this a change you wish to see?
State it now.

25.
PEACEFUL PASSAGE

MEETING POINT

I was placed in another situation I would like to share, and for those of you who are getting on in years, I ask you to truly hear what is being called for. I speak not on behalf of "me." I speak on behalf of "we."

I took part in an experimental facility of change in which these new yet timeless codes for care were being practiced. The opportunity arose to bring into our circle a man in his final days who had suffered a stroke, was in a wheelchair, and had dementia. I clearly recognized the man as a brother from the past. I agreed at this time to assist his soul to move with the transition from Earth to the higher planes, and that's how he came to be in our midst.

PATH OF BETRAYAL

In this lifetime, this great man had not walked a life of greatness. In fact, it was the opposite. I cannot discuss the details. However, let me say clearly to you this was a great man regardless of what had come to pass.

He, like many of us, had experienced lifetimes of severe separation so that we could come back to our truth. Many of us out there walk the path of betrayal to others in ways that we may not like to speak of. In fact, some of us have perpetrated the unspeakable. Truth be told, we all have in one lifetime or another.

SINS OF THE PAST

And so, with this man, we returned to the fields of creation so that he could harness what life force remained in order to view his own soul's contract for this lifetime and make remarkable shifts to line up with The One. Cared for by some of the most beautiful people that I have yet to know, his physicality sat with facilitators as his mind sat with God.

He would speak to me in complete cognition as soon as we entered a meditative space. His soul showed me the karma that he wanted to disentangle before he passed from the Earth plane. While he could not remember my name, who I was, what day it was, or where he was, he would unload the regrets of his past with precision so that his soul could feel the grief that he had inflicted or that had been inflicted upon him.

PEACEFUL TRAJECTORY

As each day passed, he would turn within and ensure that his heavenly body was matching up to where he wanted to turn. His internal radar was alive and well. His ability to discern truth from fiction was much more than what anyone recognized.

And so it went that we would connect in the eternal planes and move closer to a peaceful voyage.

INVASION

However, when it came down to it, I was too weak to handle the invasion that was taking place. For this time and space were being shattered by those who were intent on keeping his soul and dissuading my own. While I tried, I could not make the difference that I intended at that time, for the backup methods I had called for were not fully in place. I still had to learn, as did he.

MAKING AMENDS

These people, these souls who are at the edge of death's doorway, are asking for this last reprieve. They wish to be heard. They wish to be acknowledged, and they wish for a way out. They know that confession is their ultimate savior, and they know that it is not to a priest that it must be done. They know that truly it is to their own Self that they must make amends with. However, sometimes they do not know the way.

FORGIVING THE SELF

And because for each and every one of us, a resting place will eventually be called for, there is an opportunity to present great change for the passing process. Yet, we know not what we look for when we confess our "sins". We know not that when we talk to God, we talk to the Self, and so the case must be made that we are not asking for forgiveness from the outside in. We are asking for forgiveness from the inside out.

Here is where we find the inner peace that the Self calls for.

And so, the space for transitional systems is calling. Let death be a doorway to freedom, not a passageway to hell.

Ah siu ma sia tai ah na, siu ma sia.
Where will your doorway lead?

CONCLUSION

THE GOLDEN AGE

I present to you, on behalf of mankind, a taste of what can occur if we together make the change back to the utopian society that once was. It is coming again as the pendulum swings; the dichotomy will be no more, and as a society, we will find a balanced approach. We are returning to the promised land, the land that many of us call home.

For those of you who know this Golden Age from the depths of your soul's calling, the entirety of mankind asks you to come forth as there is work to be done.

YOU ARE THE KEY

Commit to yourself, commit to your families, commit to your nations, and first and foremost, commit to your heart, as the restoration of the heart is what will lead to the timelines anew.

Integrate the shadow of the Self, for within the One lies both darkness and light. The unwanted noise that is produced within your own holographic field must be seen, must be heard, and must be given its voice. Embrace each part of your personal and collective existence in whatever form it takes, because rejection is where havoc ensues. The unwanted will continue its demand to be seen, for its right to existence is just as valid as any other.

SELF-REALIZATION

We live in a reality of expansion and contraction. Both are distinct forms of expression that, without each other, would not exist. Recognizing that the monsters that you seek to evade are also a part of The All is a foothold to set you free.

GUIDELINES FOR THE HEART

Look squarely in the eyes of society's shadows and call them home. If boundaries need to be set, set them firmly. Use justice as your guide, but not your ruler. Measure not what occurs in this society as the end all and be all, for the timelines untold also hold the answers.

Protect the innate goodness of man's soul and free yourself from suffering so those around you may also find peace.

Restore your ecosystem personally and planetary, for your care of the Self, the Other, and the Earthly Mother will guide you through the storm.

THE SHIFT

Yes, we are going through a purging on this planet. Yes, we are going through a cleanse. Yes, the Earth is rebelling for the land and the ancestors who have graced her planes continue to be mistreated. (Let them speak to you; they will tell you their discontent and why they now rise.)

Yes, we are going through a gateway into a multi-dimensional reality. Yes, we are seeing the greatest awakening that mankind has ever had. Yes, we are bearing witness to the collapse of the old systems that cannot keep up with the ascension frequencies of planet Earth, and yes, there are also opposing forces at work.

TOGETHER WE RISE

We must break these loops, and the way that we do this is together. It is not an overnight process. It is not a process for the faint of heart, and it is not a process for everyone on this planet. For those of you who do hear the call, it is time to reunite. It is not the first time that we have walked together, and it will not be the last.

The coding that is destined for mankind's greatness to shine through once again is available, and all we must do is get to work.

Led by the God Force that creates worlds and the entire essence of mankind as One, this is a path that is blessed.

However, the road may not be all roses, as when one confronts one's demons head-on, one must be willing to walk the path less traveled. In this, we each find the gold.

Mankind's heart is destined to be restored, and it begins with YOU.

Until the next time we meet...

Ah siu ta sia tai ah, ah siu tai ah.
May you recognise the force of God is YOU.
May you use it for its original intent.

AFTERWORD:
ALTERING THE FABRIC OF HUMANITY THROUGH TIMELINE THERAPY

Residing in the present moment has much more weight than we can possibly imagine, for everything exists, and nothing exists at all times. This is a discussion of timelines and how they affect the portrayal of the whole.

This chapter has been written four months after the rest of this book. It has been a missing link, both in my own life and that of restoring the coding of the Creator.

Each one of us carries these individual DNA threads that run through not only the physicality, but through all of existence. You may find that a farfetched thought, but in actuality, time is not linear. Time is a composite of all that is overlapped in fractal form through the strands of our DNA. We express our DNA linearly in these time/space realms, but the truth is, it is all occurring at once… and occurring not at all.

Due to this expression within the gene codes and sequences, we have the ability to alter what is and what isn't in one fell swoop. Genes are merely mirrors of "what is" within the All, expressed within the portal of time that is DNA. Think of DNA as a window into your soul that is housed within water.

When you look into the soul and find the expressions of the soul that are still in discontent, you are able to affect the DNA signature and, thus, affect the reality of the field that is expressed within the genes, and thus, the linear reality that you experience within your own life.

Do you find that you express too much hatred or anger in your existence here on planet Earth? The answer is in your gene expression. The answer to the gene expression is within your DNA. The answer to your DNA is within the time code reality locked within the ever-expanding nature of the soul.

To affect the DNA from this Earth plane, we move into timeline therapy, or it could be expressed as gene therapy, for that is the sequence that one is actually affecting with the removal of certain interferences or frequencies within the soul's timelines.

I recently had experience with this work, altering my genetic coding altogether by moving beyond the frequency of fear and into the frequency of love within the sequence of my DNA. I have experienced the love of the Creator for a number of years here on the Earth plane. However, as I have written, there were still magnetic attractions to situations that moved me from this frequency to the lower vibrational frequencies in which fear, lack, or greed were present.

I could no longer ignore the situations in which this purity of love would backfire. I would find myself in the same story of betrayal, abuse, and injustice, regardless of how pure that love remained for the Other or how clear the situations were from objective perspective. The truth is, regardless of how much I didn't buy into the victim/victimizer reality, this old-world story was occurring within my life.

I would tell myself how much I was growing and how beautiful it was to be able to assist each other in finding our way home. However, there was a missing beat. My intentions were pure, and the frequency of love stabilized, yet I would find myself at the end of a relationship, stuck in the same story. The higher my frequency, the larger and the more unexpected the fallout.

The work that I had done in addressing the shadows within my own Self and removing the rose-colored glasses of seeing everyone only as Source did not seem to be enough to shift the reflection.

Clarity, clarity, clarity, I began to demand. What is required to truly remain in the state of One? All clear questions will bring about clear answers.

Synchronicity brought about a Quantum Healing Hypnosis Therapy session, a body of work pioneered by Dolores Cannon. The premise of the work is to understand your own Self and reflect by accessing past, future, or parallel lives so that you may bring about healing and forward movement in this present reality.

The first life that I presented was my first incarnation on Earth and the moment preceding. I levitated cross-legged above a vast array of tall trees, and to my right was a long white slide that descended to a tiny strip of white sand beach bordered by a vast ocean. My feeling state was that of peace, accepting and integrating the moments before entry. I was very much in the now.

When it was time to descend, I was spun up in a grey hue, and the energy of this hue moved me to the slide. As I found my bearings on Earth and left the family of star beings that were cheering me on, I walked into life. I was there to wake up the people to their own truth. To the left, they were asleep. To the right was the same. I didn't quite know how to approach them to share the word that they were of the eternal Source, and through this knowledge, they could find the freedom that was theirs to have.

In this session, three lifetimes were presented, all of the same nature. Each time, I presented information on the eternal truth of Self. Each time, I became a martyr by the state at hand.

During this session, I wove my way through the fields of creation in order to alter the original signature that I took upon myself during the first lifetime, that of hesitation of speaking, fear of being heard, and the violent nature of death that came as a result of speaking the truth. Instead, I instilled peace. No more violence or hesitation. Only peace and everlasting joy remained once I spoke. The violence had been a natural reaction to my state as God, for the masses were not ready to see a world in which peace took the stage, in which their original capacities returned. Now, many are.

The truth is, not everyone is ready, and that is okay. The real work is only in bringing one's own Self to the truth of who they are. In this expression of the truth, all those who you encounter who are ready to see the truth will begin their own natural expansion process.

It is not up to any one of us to demand a new timeline on Earth. It is up to us all. When we find a space in which peace and acceptance can rule our own internal nature, then we will bring about the Heaven on Earth reality that we all so very much consciously want. Each one of us who embraces our truth and embarks upon the reflection of Self will bring about a cascade of events to alter the very fabric of the events to unfold on planet Earth.

The secret to altering our collective destiny is to access the space in between, otherwise known as the present moment, the now, and to bring about a revolution so fierce that no one will challenge it. This revolution is based purely on the essence of the truth of who you are, that which is the eternal form of love.

APPENDIX:
A BRIEF LOOK AT RESTORING THE WATER MOLECULE

Water has the ability to alter its structure quite easily if the person's belief can match water's inherent intent. Water is here to flow, to guide, to fill, to be filled, and to alter the lens of human perception so that we see ourselves as vessels of Source.

Purifying, restructuring, remineralizing, enhancing, and blessing our waters can assist us in recovering our natural state as God. As we take these measures, we begin to alter the frequency gridlocks within the water molecule. Frequency is the key to recovering the totality of who we are and our innate essence.

This is a very brief look at the basics of upgrading our drinking water. A more in depth look can be found on the blog at www.lifefxlivingwater.com.

FILTRATION

There are a myriad of filtration options available for removing dissolved solids from the water supply, ranging from subpar to excellent. Be aware that fluoride is not a contaminant that most filtration is able to remove. If it is marketed as doing so, question if there is a decrease in the rate of filtration as the filter is used. Typically speaking, at the time of writing this book, fluoride filters decrease in efficacy with every liter filtered, and those who sell these filters may not have been privy to the fine print.

Distilled and reverse osmosis options are the best, if not only, technical solutions to removing fluoride, however, they also inherently present their own problems.

Any process of subtraction will require the addition of a high-quality mineral salt.

STRUCTURING UNITS

Structuring units/vortex devices that can take the negative spin of the ions within tap water and restore them to nature's intent are also available. Structuring units mimic the flow of water in nature, enhance the body's ability to absorb water, and can be a great addition to your water filtration routine.

While many will suggest that filtration is not required if you structure water, not all internal waters are capable of holding the initial charge that structuring units provide. If the body is not able to filter these toxins through its own gateways, the water will revert to the original form pre-structuring, which can include physical pollutants, emotional outputs, and electromagnetic smog.

I would always recommend filtering first, then restructuring, for maximum results.

MINERALS FOR CLARIFYING SOUL'S INTENT

While filtration, distillation, and reverse osmosis can assist with the process of subtraction, the addition of minerals is essential. High-quality minerals will revitalize the cell membrane, spark the ignition switch within the cell's powerhouses, and assist water in hydrating and purifying the cell membrane.

Since 2020, I have been working with the Creator to develop LifeFX Living Water Droplets™, which can be added to optimized or subpar water. LifeFX Living Water Droplets™ contain a unique form of biotite minerals that cleanse, purify, and structure water. We then use light language (primordial sound) and very specific bandwidths of energy to encode the minerals with the frequencies of eternal light.

LifeFX Living Water Droplets™ can be applied across a wide spectrum — from drinking water and mineral salt baths to swimming pools and hot tubs. They extend into room clearing and aura sprays, as well as broader applications in agriculture, fisheries and aquaculture, soil remediation, wastewater treatment, and upgrading recycled water systems.

The combination of the biotite and light essences that we run within LifeFX are a potent combination to ground and stabilize, cleanse, and powerfully accelerate New Earth timelines within individuals as well as the plant and animal kingdoms.

LifeFX Living Water Droplets™ is a water purification and New Earth bridging agent and should not be used as a mineral supplement.

ANCIENT WATER SONGS

When I had my first experience working with these minerals to create LifeFX, ancient water songs returned through my soul's lineage. The minerals reminded me of how to craft the energy around water in order to advance awakening for the people who drink them.

It is a technique that many water bearers hold, and as they begin to reawaken their essence of Self, they will need not any outside source, including filtration or structuring units, to transmute energy within the water molecule.

LIFEFX LIVING WATER DROPLETS™

Until that time arrives for you and to support current water bearers on their journey, I offer LifeFX Living Water Droplets™ as an option to optimizing water's purity, structure, and energetic alignments.

The sound waves imprinted in LifeFX strengthen the vibratory resonance of your own original genetic expression as a living version of God.

LifeFX can rehydrate the cell, detoxify the physical form, power the mitochondria, and fast-track the expansion of consciousness into fifth-dimensional reality, as well as reawaken the heart.

It is a window into the soul of the oceans, the rivers, and the eternal essence of mankind. Co-created with Mother Earth and the Universal Source, LifeFX is an extraordinary gift to awaken the waters within.

Take the baseline frequency of LifeFX and imprint it with your own love, intentions, and care, or rewrite the coding completely with your own soul's design.

www.lifefxlivingwater.com

For questions, bulk orders, wholesale orders, and environmental and industrial applications of LifeFX Living Water Droplets™ please reach out via connect@lifefxlivingwater.com.

ACKNOWLEDGMENTS

Each person on this planet deserves acknowledgment. It is because of you that this book exists. It is because of you that we stand at the edge of Great Divide with the momentum to move forward. It is because of you that we will write the greatest story ever told. It is because of you that the holds upon this planet will come undone, and it is because of you that the momentum to shift the tide occurs. You truly are the gift this world requires.

To those of you who stand as the wind has our backs, thank you for hearing the call and for the courage to act upon your truth.

I acknowledge the original tribes of humanity as One and those committed to the restoration of this sovereign state.

To the Earth Mother who holds us, the ancestors and guardians of the land upon which I stand, the spirit of this current age, and the wisdom of the ever-unfolding heart, thank you for the opportunity to share your voice and vision. May the words that have been written reflect the purity of your intent.

To my non-incarnate support team – ah sia tai ah na siu na sia. It's been a long road. Thank you for the support, comfort, and wisdom along the way.

To my children, thank you for holding a mirror to my own heart. May your lives be blessed as you have blessed mine.

Dear Dad, words cannot express my appreciation for your unconditional, loving support through the growing pains to arrive at who I am today.

ABOUT THE AUTHOR

In early 2020, after fifteen years on a spiritual awakening journey, Zhara J. Mahlstedt experienced an instantaneous remembrance of her soul lineage. She recalled the original "fall of man," the key to overcoming obstacles on the Earth plane, and the sounds of creation — the original harmonics of the Universe. This particular light language reactivates the original Source coding within the DNA, clears false imprints from the human design, and opens portals for timeline shifts.

Over her lifetime, Zhara has been trained by her spirit team for this pivotal moment in Earth's history, when mankind will recognize its place in the greater galactic community. She has navigated the various planes of existence to gain a deep understanding of the challenges that this planet and species face, and the solutions that are required.

Zhara frames life on Earth from a perspective that enables us to remember that our individualized aspects are part of the same Source. She helps people see beyond the divisions that exist within society and within their own hearts, so they may reunite with the love that they are.

She has found the integration of the Self in the acknowledgment that each one of us, regardless of who we are, is a fractal of the Source, and the Source holds pure love without judgment of any expressions on the Earth plane. She is a channel for higher consciousness and transmits information and energy from the primordial realms, in which there is no division, only space.

Serving in this lifetime as a psychic channel, spiritual guide, and mentor, Zhara's mission is to restore the original genetic sequence to the cell. A lifelong student, she is committed to the restoration of the Earth and mankind. Her services, which include weekly group calls, and additional resources can be found on her website, *reignitingthesoulspark.com*.

Zhara hosts two podcasts: *Reigniting the Soul's Spark*, focused on moving through spiritual awakening into enlightenment, and *The Dragon Diaries,* aimed at supporting spiritually advanced youth. These are accessible on various platforms including her website, YouTube, Spotify, and Apple Podcasts.

LifeFX Living Water Droplets™ is her offering to assist mankind and Mother Earth in cleansing, remineralising, and reawakening the waters. More information is available at *lifefxlivingwater.com*.

Connect with her on social media platforms including YouTube, Instagram, Facebook and Telegram @zharajmahlstedt @reignitingthesoulspark @lifefxlivingwater.

www.ingramcontent.com/pod-product-compliance
Lightning Source LLC
Chambersburg PA
CBHW062036290426
44109CB00026B/2644